# INDUSTRY 5.0 AND DATA ECONOMY

# INDUSTRY 5.0 AND DATA ECONOMY

Precursor to Embracing ESG and AI led transformation

**Anirban Bhattacharyya**
Cristina Dolan

Vitasta

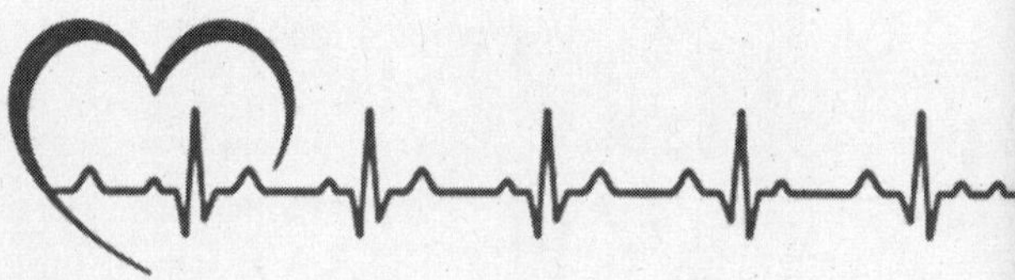

To
Mahendra Soni, my brother-in-law,
who suffered a massive heart attack
this year on 4 March

Published by
Renu Kaul Verma
Vitasta Publishing Pvt Ltd
4348/4C, Ansari Road, Daryaganj
New Delhi - 110 002
info@vitastapublishing.com

ISBN: 978-81-19670-20-8

First Edition 2024
MRP ₹425



Edited by Prof Alka Gupta
Typeset by Rohit Gautam
Cover Design by Somesh Kumar Mishra
Printed by Chaman Enterprises, New Delhi

# Contents

# Preface

As we embrace the most challenging time of our life, to make the planet a better place to live, we need to empower us with certain techniques, strategies and best practices to manage climate crises and the risk associated with it. Understanding the field of climate management, social management and governance towards the best practices is a daunting task. Every organisation, every business unit within the organisation, every employee for the unit are struggling to figure out the business and execution strategies. Enabling these strategies towards a successful transformation consumes time, takes a lot of organisational change and leadership effectiveness. Our book on Data Economy and Leadership transformation is the step one towards enabling a new normal way of facing the new challenge of climate crisis.

Climate crisis is not the only challenge. Bringing in diversity, equity and inclusion (DEI) in the transformation mix is and will be a critical factor to fight the climate challenge. While we are focusing on global warming, bringing in right mindset with people is critical. We need to bring people together to fight the global warming. This book is a recipe towards enabling the theory of change for leaders at the helm of the organisations. Right mix of intuitive and non-intuitive decision making will be very critical. Decision making needs facts and data. As we all know, data is the biggest asset on earth nowadays. Hardly being used and analysed, especially for climate change purposes, DEI purposes and policies to be rolled out, data is the most powerful entity for an organisation. It not only sets the stage to define top goals of the leaders but also this creates a new revenue model. Enabling new revenue models with data and AI is one of the biggest transformation agenda for the leaders. The constant tussle between digital transformation and the need for full business automation needs resolution cards, decision making power through platform led mindset and lastly evaluating if this would harm the planet by bringing too much automation which in turn emits carbon. Enabling the right business model will be critical. This book addresses various facts and facets of these transformation agenda.

Business models are changing. Industry lines are blurring. With Industry 5.0 being here, it will be very important to be agile for enabling the whole value chain for achieving success. Success is nothing but having a happy customer, a happier balance sheet and the happiest mother earth.

What is the Strategy in the era of AI and Sustainability? Enjoy the book on connecting all the dots between leadership, data and ESG.

Chapter 1

# Economic Fundamentals and the Data Economy

Understanding the Data Economy first requires an introduction, best done by digging into the history of an economy. The etymology of the word is originally from the Greek *eco*, which means house, and *nomos* or *nemein*, which means to account, or to manage. Later in the fifteenth century, *économie*, derived from Old French and Latin, represented the increasing relevance of the management of material resources. Usage to represent the housed management of a 'country's' accounts began in the 1600s–the language parallels developing need.

There is a substantial body of science measuring the economies of countries including the Gross Domestic Product (GDP) and the growth rate year-over-year. Today, the definition of an economy points to the production, distribution, and consumption of goods and services.

However, understanding how to represent the economic value generated through the use or sharing of data in a financial statement is not as mature as other asset classes. Data as an asset class is generated and consumed throughout countries and organisations, and at times improperly cleaned and stored– which of course prevents optimal value creation. Simultaneously, technology has played a major role in national-level economic growth, as evidenced by the GDP per capita growth rates around the world in the graph below.

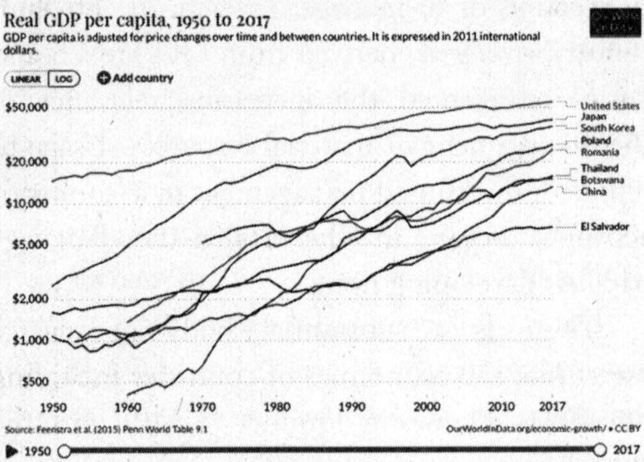

Since 1870, GDP in the United States economy has grown on an average of 1.83 per cent per year, entirely driven by technological innovation. Each of the Industrial Revolutions has introduced new types of technologies that created dramatic efficiencies. The commercial manufacturing of soap and washing machines freed up crucial hours of labour that were consumed by cleaning. As technology created more leisure time, it opened the opportunity for new industries, like entertainment and national sporting events.

Growth is being driven by technology and data, especially for less developed countries, at a much faster pace. South Korea had one of the largest economic transformations over the past 60 years, from an agricultural economy, to being one of the top ten exporters in the world with the 11th largest economy based on GDP. This growth was driven by technological innovation and the use of information for efficiency, and South Korea's R&D expense as a percentage of GDP is higher than that of any other country.

Data as an element of the technology frontier that is generated by networked technologies and consumed by systems to create new business models helps grow GDP. The cognitive use of data is transformative, and the systems that can be powered by data driven or data led innovations can provide life changing services at a price point not possible without technology.

Now, the value of digital and intangible information outweighs the value of tangible values. A 2017 CFA Institute blog post states that the 'the market value of S&P 500 Index companies is attributed to intangible assets that are largely not reflected in those companies' financial statements.' The value of intangible assets is not appropriately recorded on balance sheets, and the value creation is not reflected

**GDP per capita, 1820 to 2016**

Our World in Data

GDP per capita adjusted for price changes over time (inflation) and price differences between countries - it is measured in international-$ in 2011 prices.

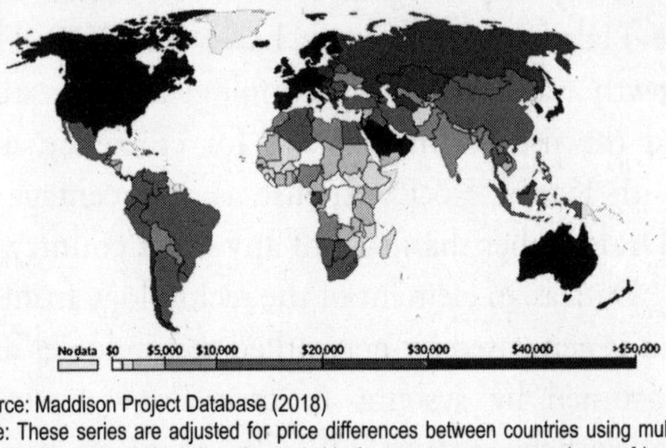


Source: Maddison Project Database (2018)
Note: These series are adjusted for price differences between countries using multiple benchmark years, and are therefore suitable for cross-country comparisons of income levels at different points in time.

in the financial statements: The five largest companies on the S&P 500 index have $21.3 trillion or intangible assets and only $4 billion in tangible assets. Most interesting is how fast the value of intangible assets is growing compared to tangible assets.

The big question: How will the 'data' get accounted for as a value generating asset that will accelerate growth in the next decade? While data is just a portion of what is 'intangible assets', the category has grown to be more than $57 trillion globally according to the Global Intangible Finance Tracker.

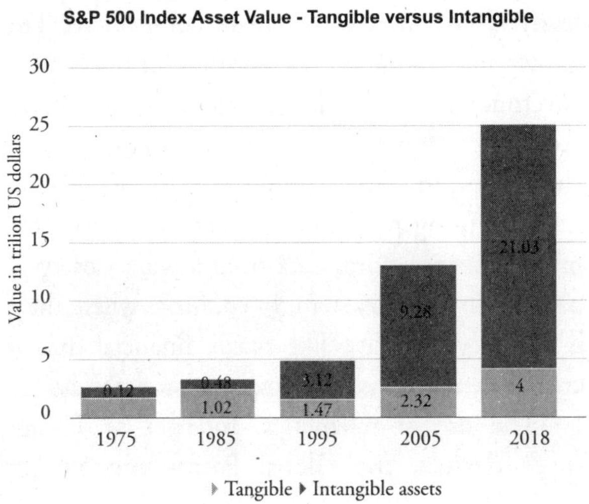

Understanding the value of data requires understanding the economics used to determine value creation. An example of intangible and digital assets growing economies can be seen in the Brazil, Russia, India, and South Africa (BRICS), where global supply chain management driven by data enables optimisation. Growth in the leading emerging markets, which include Brazil, Russia, India, China, and South Africa have accelerated by utilising global data driven strategies in the automation of supply chain processes like transportation, fulfillment, and warehouse management.

These traditional industries require data from many global sources to remain competitive. The growth of these industries is critical for the BRICS governments to experience long-term sustainable economic growth. Every step in the supply chain process from purchasing, procurement, manufacturing, production, inventory, and material management requires data from a wide variety of partners in the ecosystem. In countries where there is currency volatility, like Brazil, financial data is critical to reduce risk and improve profitability.

The use of telematics, Internet of Things (IoT) devices, the Global Positioning System

(GPS), and external data sources, like weather data, can improve transportation costs, which for some products can be more than 50 per cent of the product expense. Inefficiencies in how the data is shared creates barriers. Yet in some countries, the flow of data between the members of ecosystems is hindered by the complexity of the laws. For example, the new evolving trade war between the United States and China, presents new concerns for Multinational Corporations (MNCs) regarding the Encryption Law of the People's Republic of China which prohibits the use of foreign encryption items.

This not only impacts the ability to share data with suppliers, customers, and distributors, it also makes communicating with business operations in China over a network problematic.

### The Blocking of Cross-Border Data Flows

Many countries block the use and flow of certain kinds of local data outside their countries for a variety of reasons.

In September 2020, Ireland's privacy regulator issued a preliminary order ordering Facebook to stop transferring European consumer data to the United States. China's new encryption laws may create issues for local foreign multinational organisations with business operations that utilise the Chinese infrastructure and networks.

The two images are from the Information Technology and Innovation Foundation report.

The first image shows the level of data constraints for countries. The second image is a graph that shows the different types of data that are blocked, which can vary from country to country. Some countries prohibit information about customers and their transactions from leaving the country. In August 2020, Ireland's Data Protection Commission ordered Facebook to stop the data transfer of information about its European users to the United States. This was the first move taken by the EU regulators to enforce the new European Schrems II data ruling.

While Facebook and other companies may argue that users have opted-in to share their data, the new ruling could also impact European startups which may not be able to use US cloud providers or run their operations in the cloud across different time zones.

The rules for data usage vary from country to country, and in some cases like the United States, the rules could vary from state to state when it

## Blocking the Global Flows of Data

### Which Countries Block Data Flows?*

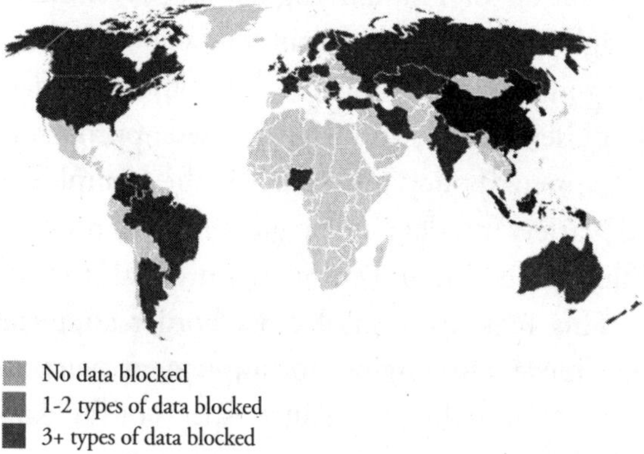


### What Types of Data Are Blocked?*

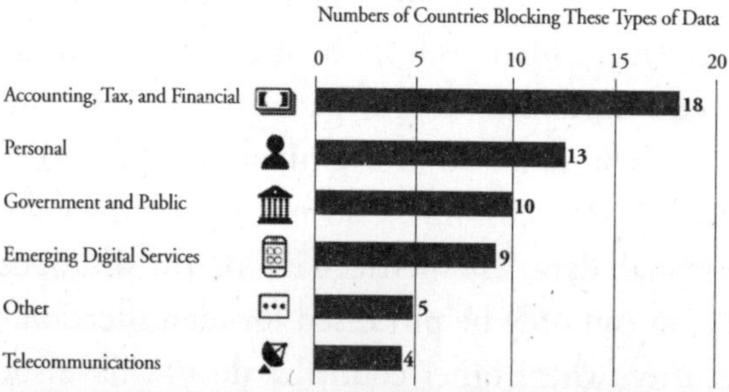


Learn more at itif.org/databarries

comes to a person's personal data. The United Nations has worked on the right to data privacy and free expression as part of the Universal Declaration of Human Rights, as governments struggle to determine the rules in a continuously changing digital landscape. The objective is to use a User-Centric and Rights Based approach to government policy on data, yet the complexity and variety of data on a global basis make it difficult to define and enforce a universal strategy.

This makes universal cross border strategies even more challenging to implement without understanding the compliance aspects of the data. In addition to the variations in data regulations by geography, there are variations in how different types of data are regulated. Healthcare data has different regulations from financial data, although in the European Union, patients and customers own their data. In the United States, patients and banking customers do not legally own their personal data. Biometric data in the European Union can only be processed for identification or security, where other countries do not have such restrictions.

### Aggregators Provide Critical Data Powering Businesses Media

There are several major data aggregators that collect local citation information about local businesses including business name, address, phone number, website, and other business details. This information is also validated by other companies like telephone companies and the US Post office. This data is then used by numerous online publishers. As of January 2020, Infogroup, Localeze and Factual are dominant data aggregators that offer the data to major websites. Data is typically sourced from multiple sources and compared, to verify the data for accuracy, which can be expensive.

### Financial Services

Data aggregation is critical to financial services. Without it, financial leaders would not have the information needed to assess risk. Traders—especially high-speed traders and quants—would not have the information necessary to successfully generate profits from data led or data driven trades. The profitability of these types of financial businesses that are driven by data makes the critical information used to fuel the growth extremely valuable.

In January 2020, Visa acquired Plaid Financial for $5.3 billion, a company that offers data piped through Application Programming Interfaces (APIs) that provide access to financial data within customers financial accounts. This critical customer financial data drives financial transactions that provide revenue and growth for some of the largest financial unicorns.

Capital markets are driven by financial markets, and there are numerous firms involved in the delivery of different types of data. International Securities Identification Number (ISIN) codes are used to tie together everything from pricing and real-time trades to news. As financial instruments have become more complex, the use of data has become even more critical. Financial firms pay large sums for data to gain insights on trades, for example satellite images of parking lots can help traders predict sales for a quarter. Sentiments, gained from specialised websites, can help pharmaceutical companies determine the appetite for a new drug.

### Sustainability

One of the most critical metrics for public companies is centered around sustainability.

Applying Design Thinking to manufacturing will transform many different facets of the business from production processes, supply chain strategies, technology adoption, business models and even the culture of an organisation.

Cost-effective production in a circular economy requires a different approach towards sustainable manufacturing. The use of intelligent technologies reduces the product development cycle and costs and facilitates on demand additive manufacturing. Cross-border data is central to every component of this process.

### Healthcare

Healthcare data is highly regulated and siloed. In Europe, patients own their data, although this is not the case in the United States. While there is tremendous value in utilising cancer data for precision medicine, it is difficult to access the data for analysis due to the way healthcare data is regulated and protected by financial institutions. Hackers value healthcare data because if patient records can be obtained and utilised to illegally buy pain medications, it can be highly profitable.

Harvard Professor Michael Porter developed a Value-Based Health Care framework for restructuring health care systems to measure value creation and drive improved patient outcomes. Many healthcare service providers are compensated based on the value created and the outcomes, which motivates providers. The ability to measure improved outcomes is based on data within the healthcare system, and it is the basis of compensation in contracts. The healthcare system is an example of how the data within the network can help drive improvements in outcomes and increased compensation.

***

Chapter 2

# An Essential History of Data

The collection of data has fueled transformation of economies since the beginning of human civilisation. It is a powerful tool in enabling quantifiable understanding, while powering the management of change. Programmes for counting the population, production, and resources by governments go as far back as the first known census during the Babylonian Empire in the thirty eighth century BC. Governments have executed census programmes throughout history to extract insights for rulers to understand population growth and resource consumption, while becoming the established basis for taxation. Detailed records from the Chinese Han Dynasty in second century AD and the Book of Numbers from the fifth century records are available today.

The Library of Alexandria in ancient Egypt attempted to archive the largest collection of data from the era, until it was destroyed in the year forty eighth century AD by the Romans.

Tools for data collections have grown in sophistication over time, from early clay tablets inscribed in cuneiform more than 5800 years ago, to the simple system of knots and strings used by the Incas in the fifteenth century. Computing devices from the early abacus were used by the Sumerians about 4500 years ago and later used throughout Asia and Europe. Innovations like the punch card driven Tabulating Machine, created in 1890 by Herman Hollerith, enabled the systematic calculation of census data recorded on punch cards in 18 months, a task which typically took about 7 years to process into a final report.

The timeless expression, "knowledge is power" is attributed to English philosopher Sir Francis Bacon, one of the founders of scientific method. He stated that scientific knowledge could improve human life and argued for the need of scientific method. It is not simply the data alone that provides knowledge, data has no value without strategy.

### The Ancient Art of Representing Data

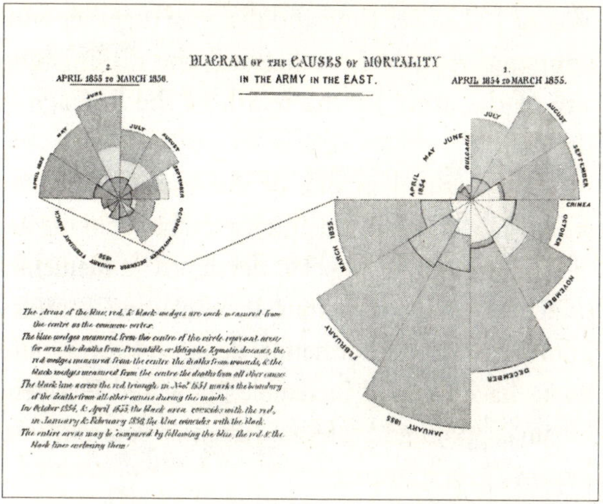


Source: National Library of Medicine

One early statistician utilising data visualisation was Florence Nightingale, who provided insights on factors attributed to death during the Crimean War. Most important were her pioneering innovations in data collection, and her ability to present data in an intuitive way via a coxcomb pie chart, where the colours and segment sizes helped provide a visual approach, explaining the factors contributing to mortality at the British military hospital in Turkey in 1856.

Additionally, the famous 1869 statistical graphic map by Charles Joseph Minard that charts Napoleon's march to Moscow during the War of 1812 over time and distance together with temperature, cleverly represents the diminishing size of the army by the width of the line across the map.

It is featured in one of the books written by retired Yale Prof Edward Tufte, a trailblazer in the use of data for storytelling. He developed fundamental principles and innovations in visualising complex information and information design. His work and books have received incredible praise and President Obama appointed Professor Tufte to a committee to improve govt transparency.

**Napoleon's March to Moscow, The War of 1812**

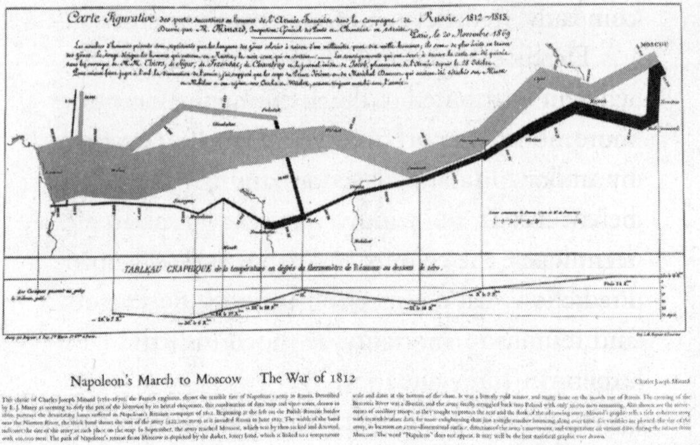


Source: Britannica

**Strategic Use of Data Throughout History**

Throughout history, military operations have utilised data to understand risks and create strategies with the resources that are available. Today, there are many different technologies that provide continuous sources of data for governments that go beyond satellite imagery, sensors, weather, geomagnetic fluctuations, drones, inventories, personnel files, and internet traffic that enable situational awareness for decision making. It is not just about the data or the ability to plot the data, it is about the context. Cyberwarfare is an example of how valuable data and connectivity have become to nations, and predictive analytics are used by security agencies and insurance companies to understand and reduce risks.

Elections are numbers-driven campaigns wherein poll results have altered strategies. The more modern use of big data, to micro target voters by utilising data analysts that model predictive behaviours and apply internet marketing techniques, can be seen in several elections. Predictions modeled from behaviour, support, and responsiveness scores are used together with experiments to validate the theories.

Campaigns can obtain data sets from the United States Elections Project official voter files maintained by Secretaries of State and merge them with other data sets that indicate education levels and other financial information. (Most people do not realise that the voting history of individuals is public information, while only the actual vote is private.)

A seminal Harvard research paper, Political Campaigns and Big Data, by David Nickerson and Todd Rogers, shows the prediction results for candidate support over three consecutive presidential elections in Ohio, created by Catalist, LLC, a consulting firm and political data vendor with a unified national voter database that only works with Democrats, Progressives, and non-profit issue advocacy organisations. The work changed the targeting strategy, toward persuasion modeling and mobilising democratic voters that were not likely to vote.

The MIT Technology Review wrote a series of articles on Obama's use of data on the science behind the Obama presidential campaign, which was led by Dan Wagner, the Chief Analytics officer for Obama in 2012—headed up by a team of data scientists referred to as the "Cave". Data derived from voter registration records, past campaigns and other consumer data were used to create predictive scores at the individual level. The team carefully correlated the enhanced voter data with the media channels to target cost effective campaigns at the persuadable voters.

In the famous case of Cambridge Analytica, a subsidiary of London based SCL Group, data from over 50 million Facebook users was collected through a paid and sponsored application called "thisisyourdigitallife", which was created by Aleksandr Kogan, a University of Cambridge psychologist, that claimed to be utilising the data for academic research.

Whistleblower Christopher Wylie revealed how the use of data violated Facebook's 2015 policy which disabled the ability to target friends of engaged users, resulted in Facebook suspending the firms involved. The claim was made that psychographic models of Facebook users were being created to exploit vulnerabilities and access their networks.

### Data All Around Us

The use of data to understand and predict has become a growing part of our world. Yet to understand the transformational power of data, it is critical to understand the evolution of enabling technology, and the drivers that are creating new opportunities and powering new business models, that offer critical services at price points and cannot be achieved without technology.

Consumers today benefit from the predictive analytics utilised by a variety of service providers to determine what products we are likely to buy, need, or enjoy. Many companies like Amazon present related products based on history, and movies are recommended by Netflix based on viewing profiles.

Consumer Behaviours have been analysed by psychologists and retailers for over a century, yet data rich eCommerce solutions offer a wealth of information, insights, and actions not achievable through retail stores. Understanding the customer journey, and the phases of researching, engaging, and transacting are much more transparent through online platforms. Email targeting platforms have evolved into Inbound Marketing platforms, like HubSpot, which provides customer insights throughout the buyer's journey, and offers the tools to convert potential customers into sales at different points throughout the customer experience.

There are over 200,000 datasets at DATA.gov that can be extracted and analysed. The New York Metropolitan Transportation Authority (MTA) makes aggregated data for traffic over bridges and tunnels available through the data.ny.gov website. While traffic tickets are now issued automatically from automatic plate detection, image capture and analysis, quick decisions can be made to improve congestion and public transportation. Travel times, weather related safety and even pollution levels can be obtained for effective problem solving or policy creation.

### Drivers and Milestones

The 1st Industrial Revolution kicked off an economic shift as power machines emerged and people moved from farms to the city. Although there were multiple negative effects because of the rapid urbanisation of cities that grew with lack of planning, infrastructure or sanitation, there were several social benefits which included the mechanisation of agriculture, improvements in railroads and communications.

The Technological Revolution, also known as the 2nd Industrial Revolution, was powered by electricity, petroleum, and communications technologies. Steel production enabled the growth of railways, connecting rural parts of cities, and development of skyscrapers.

The 3rd Industrial Revolution brought the rise of computers, electronics, and telecommunications. The word Artificial Intelligence (AI) was coined, and the World Wide Web emerged. The democratisation of information and the decrease in transaction costs built new business models as the digital world began to evolve. The first integrated database systems evolved in the 1960s and innovations enabled larger structured and unstructured databases.

Within the 3rd Industrial Revolution was the evolution of the Internet. Initially, Web 1.0 provided mostly static pages. With the evolution of Web 2.0, there was a rise in user generated content on social platforms. The most revolutionary part of the internet transformation was Web 3.0, with the introduction of the semantic web, which enabled custom content and targeted advertising. The ability for computers to understand humans through web services facilitated the growth of new applications and software agent enabled functionality like image searches. This era transformed the business models of internet companies.

As the mobile phone evolved into powerful smartphones, that are central to all personal transactions and communications, the rise of AI powered applications began. Computing power at the edge of networks with powerful processing abilities and flexible cloud computing capabilities enabled new functionality and on-demand services.

The 4th Industrial Revolution represents the cyber physical systems and interactions between physical, digital, and biological worlds in a way that blurs the boundaries of systems and markets. This also creates the opportunity to create more immersive and cross functional solutions that extend beyond the typical company silos.

Relationships with financial firms will transform as platforms offer financing with lower friction at the point of transaction. Customers are greeted with custom services that reflect their preferences to improve customer loyalty. Technology enabled partner services are seamlessly provided throughout value chains, enabling companies to partner in new ways which increase sales and customer satisfaction more cost effectively.

Platforms today are transitioning into financial services, for example, lending by Square Capital or Amazon Lending offers their sellers business loans based on the transactional data

The New Industry 4.0 Data Economy

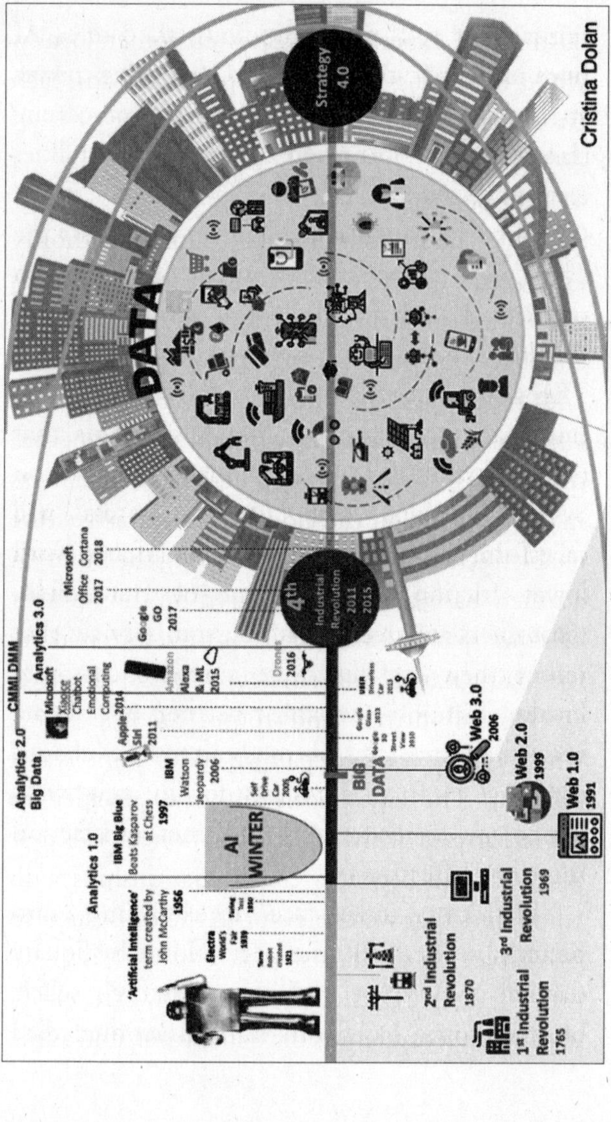

extracted from the platform, without using data from traditional credit agencies. Another popular application is Venmo, providing a money transmitter without a bank charter.

### Computer Powered Analytics

The 1970s brought databases, which were filled with cleaned and structured data in Relational Databases that enabled analysis and retrieval by utilising Sequel. The science and methodology of Data Modelling evolved, as first described by ANSI in 1975. The 1980s brought Data Warehouses, Executive Information Systems (EIS) and Decision Support Systems, also called Executive Decision Systems, which utilised highly structured data to provide business insights through a dashboard. Deep analysis of business goals through an interface powered by Online Analytical Processing (OLAP) utilising multidimensional data enabled complex analyses of structured data and correlated datasets. The ability to utilise data and technology for the creation of actionable strategies launched the field of Business Intelligence.

Data mining evolved in the 1990s to extract patterns and insights from large volumes of diverse datasets. Traditional Predictive Analytics have been used for decades by companies interested in performance and profits, although through Machine Learning and AI the space has grown from what was originally just straightforward statistics. Prescriptive Analytics utilises statistics, machine learning and AI in analysing raw data to generate models and determine outcomes. Gartner defines Descriptive Analytics as the use of data to analyse historic performance through manual or traditional business intelligence processes along with visualisations of the data.

The internet introduced large volumes of distributed small data, which was the catalyst that transitioned into the world of Big Data in the early 2000s. Hadoop marked a milestone that enabled the processing of large datasets that were growing exponentially at high speeds in a variety of different formats. The data storage in the Cloud and Data Lakes enables repositories for a variety of unstructured or raw state data types.

The application of a more holistic approach of analysis, that involves different technologies from AI to semantics for the improvement or emulation of human-like intelligence with a level of adaptability and learning is Cognitive Analytics (CA). The CA offers the ability to enable adaptive decision making and advanced customer services through an ongoing learning process using new types of Enterprise Cognitive Systems.

### The Phases of Analytics

The Harvard Business Review article, Analytics 3.0, by Thomas Devenport (2013) lays out the milestones of Analytics 1.0 through Analytics 3.0 over the past seven decades, which are the subject of his book on *Competing on Analytics*. The Analytics 1.0 phase was derived from structured data stored in data warehouses. Business Intelligence was powered through pre-structured queries built around business metrics for sales and financial metrics, enabling the creation of reports and executive information dashboards. While existing tools allowed analysis focused on past performance, spreadsheets enabled the financial modeling.

The introduction of the semantic web in the Web 3.0 phase in the mid-2000s, enabled Analytics 2.0 and introduced large volumes of small data and the use of frameworks such as Hadoop and NoSQL.

This Big Data phase introduced the ability to quickly analyse large volumes of small unstructured data utilising complex queries to generate predictive views powered by new business models.

Internet companies like Google and Facebook, which dominate the targeted advertising space, pioneered what is now called Big Data. The new role of Data Scientist has evolved and become much more sophisticated. In-memory analytics offered a new level of speed in analytics.

Analytics 3.0 is described as the revolutionary process of combining the real time insights with customer specific actions. Data gathered at the edge from IoT devices, sensors, telematics, or other distributed computing devices combined with the power of decentralised analytics enables real time decision making. Customers are empowered decision makers, and their active engagement through many types of smart devices can frame new types of descriptive, predictive, and prescriptive analytics.

The available technologies allow better, faster, and cheaper decision-making—offering enterprises the ability to increase customer satisfaction while transacting more cost-effectively and efficiently. This enables personalised services that would be less cost effective in the absence of technology, for example the use of telemedicine to extend healthcare services to remote locations.

### Data Management Maturity Model

In August of 2014 the CMMI Institute, a wholly owned subsidiary of Carnegie Mellon University, released the first version of the Data Management Maturity (DMM) Model, which evolved from Carnegie Mellon's Software Engineering Institute (SEI) and was sponsored by Microsoft, Lockheed Martin, and Booz Allen Hamilton. The model was created as a foundation for business results that were based on trusted data and enabled improved decisions, increased efficiencies, and decreased costs, while adhering to regulatory compliance. It is a reference model framework of best practices for fundamental data management practices and is not focused on a specific technology, architecture, or data modelling.

### Growth of Data

It is calculated that in 2003, there was 5 billion Gigabytes of data, and in 2011 that same amount was created every two days. By 2013, the same amount was created every 10 minutes.

In 2012, the Guardian published a story 'Study: less than 1 per cent of the world's data is analysed, over 80 per cent is unprotected' with insights from several studies on Big Data. One study by Digital Universe reported that only 0.5 per cent of global data is analysed. A study by International Data Corporation (IDC) and sponsored by EMC estimated that only 3 per cent of data was tagged and only 0.5 per cent was used for analysis.

A Bloomberg article reported in 2015, '96 per cent of businesses fail to unlock data's full value'. While three quarters of the organisations surveyed lacked the skills to extract the data, it is clear there is a need for a strategy to understand and unlock the value in the data.

An Experian data quality study, the 2017 global data management benchmark report, stated that only 18 per cent of organisations have a data strategy, while only 44 per cent of organisations trust their data to make important decisions and C-Level executives believe that 33 per cent of their organisational data is inaccurate.

## THE CROSSOVER INTO THE TRANSFORMATIVE ERA OF DATA

### 1) The Creation of Value from Data

This is where the 4$^{th}$ Industrial Revolution begins, at the point where the data and smart devices throughout the network can be used to power new models that transcend traditional businesses or siloed markets.

2) **The Growth in Data Value**
According to a 2019 Intangible Assets Financial Statement Impact Comparison Report by AON Insurance and the Ponemon Institute, the value of intangible assets was $21 trillion dollars in the US. Intangible Assets represents 84 per cent of the S&P 500 value, which also includes IP rights and reputation, is now worth substantially more than the property, plant, and equipment assets of firms. Web 3.0 and the semantic web influenced the growth of Big Data which is defined by the Volume, Variety, Velocity and Veracity. Extracting value from the Big Data goes beyond just the ontologies and relationships between entities that fueled the semantic web.

3) **Servitization**
Transformation from Products to Solutions: The concept of 'Servitization' goes back to the late 1980s, and yet it is the more recent availability of sensors, IoT devices, AI, robotics, and other smart devices capable

of producing or analysing data at the edge of networks that is powering innovation to create a competitive advantage and strengthen customer relationships.

Servitization enables product companies to become more competitive by expanding their offering with services. Basic repair and operational use information is communicated to facilitate smoother operations and less downtime.

The contractual agreements with customers are streamlined with extended contracts which share the business risk over longer extended product life cycles. Different ownership and use of business models evolve over time, shifting the make-up of the product organisations.

Data drives the ability to deliver better services, with a focus on the outcomes and not on the maintenance of equipment. Partnering with customers on the success of their business locks out competitors with a higher level of customer intimacy that is sustainable through good and bad economies. Product companies can transform into businesses offering continuous services and not just the sale of a base produce with spare parts or repairs. This is a more resilient business model for product companies, and helps customers achieve business success. Data and insights consumed by cognitive agents enable problems solving in seconds, which prevents customer downtime and revenue loss.

**Blurring the Lines with Partnerships**

Leveraging financial services transparently throughout customer journeys or servitization, enables more efficient transactions, better customer service and increased margins. Financial partners benefit from lower cost customer acquisition, while the service provider decreases the friction of completing customer transactions, making it a win-win for partners, customers, and service providers.

The growth beyond just Software-as-a-Service to Products-as-a-Service is changing industries from the consumer automobile industry and manufacturing to financial services. It is facilitated by the ability to rent out regulatory licensing and the financial plumbing as-a-service from banks like Cross River, Celtic or Evolve, decreases the time to launch a new financial business or service within an existing platform. Instead of spending months to meet with financial institutions to negotiate a contract, the services can be initiated on demand.

***

Chapter 3

# The Evolution in Data Use

The expression 'data is the new oil' by Mathematician Clive Humby in 2006 has been amplified over the years by companies, entrepreneurs, and the media. Yet, 60 per cent of companies have dark data levels as high as 50 per cent or more according to Splunk. Gartner defines dark data as information assets that are collected through traditional business activities, that are not utilised or analysed to build value for the organisation.

Data has traditionally been a cost centre, although there may be compliance requirements for gathering some of the dark data, the transition to convert data into a profit centre is what is powering the new data economy. This is a dramatic shift from the traditional analysis of data that has been practiced for years to simply understand trends or make predictions. Extracting wisdom from data requires going beyond just utilising statistical methodologies.

Appreciating the value of data has increased as the ability to extract wisdom from data and not just insights has made data more actionable and valuable to businesses. The noise levels in data can be high, making it a challenge to extract actionable value from the data.

The generation of data by a variety of different devices and siloed systems, as an entity or transaction travels through time and space in an ecosystem changes the dynamics and definition of systems. The network effects of these systems increase the value and use of the data within the network. While we have been hearing about the 'networked economy', it is really about the use of the data with the network that powers new business models and enables the new data economy.

Data science has been around for over 50 years, yet the ability to extract knowledge and wisdom from data to power new business models beyond the confines of an application interface is new. The nature of data and the value of the data within the appropriate context has become more popular as the use of smart networked devices has exploded. Data Science programmes for both analysts and computer science at leading universities are growing. This exponential analysis of data enables a new type of science.

### Data Science versus Data Analyst

The terms 'data scientist' and 'data analyst' are used interchangeably, yet the roles are different. A data analyst will utilise data to understand trends and interpret information from a business perspective to support business decisions. It could be argued that data analysts have existed before computing enabled sophisticated analysis and data representation.

Data scientists are usually computer scientists that go beyond just analysing the data, they will clean, collect, find patterns, use algorithms, and model the data to enable data driven decision making. The term 'data scientist' has been attributed to two pioneers of data, in 2008, D.J. Patil, and Jeff Hammerbacher, who worked at LinkedIn and Facebook respectively. Dr D.J. Patil later went on to become the first US Chief Data Scientist at The White House.

### The Evolution into the Executive Suite

Technology has not always been considered central to business units or looked at as a competitive advantage. Prior to personal computers and networked distributed systems that were managed by businesses outside of the data centre, technology was centralised and did not engage directly with the business units or the executive suite. As technology evolved into smart embedded or personal devices, its role within organisations changed dramatically. Today technology is central to providing a competitive advantage by integrating into the business goals and utilising data to understand the customer journeys.

The growth of information systems as a valued business asset and a critical ingredient business today has brought technology out of the back room into the board room as executive roles have been designed to harness the value of technology and data by weaving it into the business objectives. Roles evolved specifically to manage the process associated with data analytics and technology driven strategies.

### The Chief Information Officer Role

In the mid-1980s, the Chief Information Officer

(CIO) role emerged which connected the board to the organisation's information technology and computing resources. Deloitte's report "From the Basement to the Cloud, The Role of the CIO over Four Decades", describes the early CIOs in the 1980s as technology developers and later, in the 1990s, expanded to include business objectives.

As the internet evolved, the role of CIO shifted to the integration and connectivity to distributed systems. With the rapid changes in industry standards, the role moved away from developing IT infrastructure to selecting industry standards. Data growth in the early 2000 began to play a bigger role in organisations, moving the responsibilities of the CIO to the regulatory side of data and infrastructure. Development of relationships within the organisation and with external partners increased the focus on business integration and transformation.

#### The Chief Data Officer Role

The Chief Data Officer (CDO) role moved data governance from the IT department into the front office as a strategic corporate asset, in 2002, when Capital One appointed Cathryne Clay Doss as the first CDO. The company values data and uses it to fuel a successful business that enables Capital One to differentiate potential customers and service them differently from their competitors. Although the industry questioned their original 'test and learn' methodology, the company has grown to become the fifth-largest consumer bank and the eight largest bank overall and the founder and CEO, Richard Fairbank, has maintained his position since it was founded in 1994.

While the CDO role differs based on the organisation, industry and culture, Forrester published a study in 2019 indicating that organisations with CDOs had better revenue growth with greater efficiencies in driving decision-making with a competitive advantage. The survey indicated that the role has gained a new level of acceptance with 59 per cent of enterprises and 55 per cent of small and medium sized businesses appointing a CDO.

An article from Harvard Business Review indicates that there has been some confusion around the CDO goals over the years, making it challenging for some to succeed in their roles. Initially, CDO responsibilities were first associated with financial firms where there was a need to protect and maintain privacy.

While the role of CDO has transformed as it has been adopted in a variety of industries, the focus has not transcended into creating economic value from data.

### The New Role of 'Chief Data Economy Officer'

Data alone is not valuable; stored indefinitely and not used strategically it incurs costs, and could possibly become a liability if not stored securely. Data requires a process to put it into action to extend businesses beyond the traditional boundaries of information systems. The data assets require context and the ability to extract wisdom to create a new level of economic value.

While this requires a strong understanding of the regulatory side of data across the geographies and industries, it also requires a different approach towards putting data into action as a powerful asset that enables new business models and serves customers in ways that were not feasible without data, connectivity, and technology.

These new data driven business models do not live behind a traditional application, and the data do not live in a structured database where historical trends and future predictions guide strategy within the constraints of existing systems. These new models extend beyond a company or a system, and are formed by embracing partnerships and utilising mechanisms outside of traditional information systems. Data driven businesses can offer customised and precision offerings tailored to customer needs at a point in time when they are needed in cost effective ways. The customer engagement is easier; transaction costs can speed up sales and the customer acquisition costs for partner companies can be substantially lower.

The value of creating the role of the Chief Data Economy Officer is that it enables an organisation to prioritise the goal and benefits the customer by taking a different approach. Putting the customer at the center of the strategy requires a different approach, a more empathetic approach that is massively data driven but is led by 'Design Thinking' and not by the enabling technology.

### Catalysts for Transformation: From Cost Centre to a Profit Centre

Without a Design Thinking approach the value of data cannot be extracted and the customer experience cannot be improved or even understood, it is just a cost center within an organisation.

Analytics have been evolving in complexity across areas that include descriptive, diagnostic, predictive and prescriptive analytics. New machine learning and AI tools have flourished over the past decade moving beyond big data analytics. Yet these tools and processes alone do not create value.

The Chief Data Economy Officer drives the growth of the data economy within an ecosystem by aligning the strategy with value creation. This requires a very different approach from how data is used within organisations today. The role requires an active approach to create mindshare to engage the organisation in a new way of thinking and measuring their success.

### Design Thinking and Personas as the Driver of Value Creation

Design Thinking utilises personas to create context for data, provides insights around behaviour throughout the entire customer journey. By defining the customers as symbolic fictional characters, the analysis becomes more tangible, empathetic, and understandable. These identified characteristics that define the personas need to be selected carefully to incorporate the appropriate facets to deliver the correlated insights representing the behaviour and information of ideal customers. The journeys capture data that is not confined to traditional transactional systems or interactions with a software application to enable the understanding of the entire ecosystem. The efficiency of this process that has been used for two decades makes it possible to understand customer behaviours, insights, preferences, and viewpoints.

The utilisation of personas provides contextually relevant dimensions that are not confined by the perimeter of a system or structured dataset. This approach enables utilising data captured across networks, siloed systems and throughout the whole customer journey. Understanding the demographic details, which include their environment, psychographics, profession and other personal details like their age, education levels, sex, or income levels, facilitates the understanding of different customer profiles.

### Ethically Harnessing the Value of Data

Organisational change is required to redefine the boundaries of how companies 'ethically' define their data assets, utilise data, and share data to achieve goals or establish partnerships. Most of the recent focus has been on personal consumer data, that has grown because of the semantic web and the increased use of smart devices. It was this initial growth of 'Big Data' that fueled the growth of AI and Analytics, yet organisations have large amounts of business-to-business data that remains untapped, which makes it challenging for organisations to understand the true value of the data.

The creation of the Chief Data Economy Officer role is more critical than ever before as organisations start to evaluate what data needs to be shared to achieve goals while making sure they are protecting the data assets of the organisation and the confidential insights that can be extracted from this data.

Working across the organisation and ecosystems, the Chief Data Economy Officer will need to know how to redefine the boundaries to create value from data, while also ethically protecting the value. Design Thinking enables targeted and creative collaboration across the organisation and with partners to build 'value chains' throughout organisations which requires an entirely new roadmap that is not blocked by the typical siloed divisions found in today's large organisations.

The same approach cannot be used to achieve different results, which is why design thinking is so critical to the success of the Chief Data Economy Officer. The Design Value Index, which is a portfolio of 16 public companies that utilize Design Thinking, has outperformed the S&P 500 over the past decade. This approach towards the Data Economy will encourage CEOs to embrace enablers like Blockchain, IoT and other distributed technologies, while making successful implementation possible.

***

Chapter 4

# Why Now?

Commerce has been driven into rapid digital transformation by COVID19. Data and technology are driving the evolution that is enabling a move towards an intelligent omnichannel commerce strategy. Integrated solutions from Product Information Management systems that operate in ecosystems where they pull in data from a variety of sources to improve the multi-dimensional visibility into products, are publishing information into a variety of different channels to improve customer journeys. The customer is at the centre of commerce, and advances in technologies like agent-based modeling systems provide insights on the behavior of customers within an ecosystem.

Beth Ann Kaminkow, CEO of Geometry, a

WPP company, has been an early thought leader in the digital transformation of commerce. In a prior role at Westfield, she conceived of B2B2C with the customer in the centre because the customer needs to be in the centre of the end-to-end journey, even in the B2B space.

The value is created by merging the end-to-end B-2-B journeys together with the customer at the centre. This defines the end-to-end data ecosystem. The revenue opportunities only come from this level of customer centricity.

'Creative Commerce' is evolving as the new form of media marketing as content channels are merging with ecommerce channels. For example, TikTok, Netflix, Facebook, Instagram, Amazon, and every company that is delivering online entertainment is now merging with commerce. This is a massive shift in the Media Marketing industry, where the new channels of commerce that are evolving were not considered commerce channels in the past. The move is going from transaction towards the customer experience and engagement. This transition leads to a new type of frictionless transaction more akin to content ingestion than to a buying process.

Digital transformation has been revolutionising

companies and media marketing over the past decade and is now powering a transformation in commerce. This 'commerce transformation' is creating an opportunity for greater creativity in the creation of new engaging customer experiences through data use, IoT, edge computing, machine learning and artificial intelligence. The data in these ecosystems can help make those experiences more targeted and bespoke, leading to higher conversions.

In the past, there were many theoretical discussions about what technology could offer, especially with the successful shift in the use of data rich social platforms which drove the former advertising models to new levels. The transformation of commerce, into connected environments, has unlocked the monetisation potential of social platforms, by connecting the commerce experience in new ways and enabling those platforms to deliver on the shareholder promise that helped them grow to their size. Alibaba and Amazon are examples of this commerce transformation where the interactions throughout the customer journey are completely different since they are rooted in different cultural behaviours that are reflected online.

As players in the commerce space deliver the technology stack that enables the use of data and networked intelligence, change is driven towards the rise in customer centric solutions. It is not about taking old advertising models and implementing them on the new platforms, it is about transforming the customer experience using data and technology.

In the prior generation, customer centric experiences evolved from consumer generated content, which was not controlled by the advertisers or the media companies. At first, advertisers utilised techniques they had used in prior generations of digital media instead of utilising the unique properties of the social platforms to create effective campaigns. Adoption has been slow when legacy systems are available, and partners are reluctant to change.

While digital transformation has been a focus of many large Fortune 500 companies, most of the companies have not transformed into data driven customer centric organisations. Successful transformation into a customer-centric organisation requires a different organisational structure and most companies have not taken that step.

COVID 19 has been the catalyst for accelerating change, because when customers change, organisations must react quickly to meet customers' evolving requirements. Companies that were already 'Customer Centric' or companies that had already invested in Direct-to-Consumer strategies were more successful in transforming to meet customer needs.

The WPP Open Data Platform and the Living Commerce Platform, offer a 360-degree partner programme which is utilising the combined capabilities of key technology partners, including Adobe, Amazon, Facebook, Google, IBM, Microsoft, Shopify, and Salesforce. The use of the best data and technology stacks together with artificial intelligence to deliver the most targeted and effective creative solutions for customers. The platform offers the ability to bring in data from many different sources including Nielsen and others to determine a unified media mix which can be thought of as a unified commerce channel. This includes the entertainment channels which had not been part of the traditional Omni-Channel mix in the past.

By knitting together all facets of the business, it enables a deeper understanding with longer term engagements with the customer at the centre. This opens the possibility for personalisation of customer centric experiences that demonstrate a deep understanding of the customer leading to longer and more valuable customer relationships enabled by data and technology to create more meaningful exchanges between the customer and the companies.

The success of digital native companies that have been able to adapt to customer needs more nimbly have paved the way for traditional companies to follow. Large companies have traditionally used incubators to explore ways to innovate, or they have purchased companies that have successfully innovated around some facet of the customer journey. Companies born-in-commerce are providing examples for the traditional companies that require a reboot into digital commerce.

While digital native companies are initially trail blazers, they struggle at creating that inflection point for growth and can make the same traditional mistakes other companies have made at similar stages. Amazon is an example of a digital native company that has built their platform around the customer utilising the data and learning from the customer journey. Being able to create that level of intelligent customer engagement is something that WPP is looking to offer its customers across their end-to-end journey through its Open Data Platform and the Geometry Living Commerce Platform.

Looking to the future, Commerce-as-a-Service is the next big wave, and the use of the data within this model is still being worked out by the sales and marketing teams. Some of the opportunities could include optimising the spend and decreasing costs, strategies to focus marketing spend specifically on products when they are in stock, to eliminate the possibility of driving customers to competitors' products when products are not in stock, and to target repurchasing habits that create loyalty loops. This ups the ante in the customer retention sphere since it means that the loss of a customer to a competitor is the loss of a high lifetime value.

Regardless of the approach, it is incredibly important to understand how to partner with members of the ecosystem including the consulting firms, technology companies and data providers. The Institute for Real Growth, Kantar Side of the Business, looked at the shifting role of the CMO,

CRO and CGOs. There is a return to the creative side of the CMO role, bringing in the intuitive creative thinking that is tied to the data, in a way that was not possible. The roles are changing, and the CMOs must be more renaissance and capable than they have ever been before to incorporate the data. Even the roles of the partners within the ecosystem have evolved.

Today there is less of a focus on 'owning the data' and more on how clients use the data to generate value through creative partnerships. The growing technology stack can be very intimidating and confusing for some customers, and the goal is to help create value.

### Data Fueling Customer Loyalty Loops

The Evolution of Product Information Management (PIM) Systems: Product Information Management systems are enabling stronger customer relationships from creation to loyalty and fueling the loyalty loops. The enhanced customer digital experience enables the integration of richer stories about products.

Below is an image used in an IDC report on how PIM improves the entire customer journey, powered from data available from customer touchpoints throughout the ecosystem and partners, to enhance the customer experience. COVID 19 has forced companies to transform from their traditional market stack to creative commerce stack that engaged the customer throughout the end-to-end journey This enables the loyalty loop as illustrated below, which strengthens the customer experience.

With companies offering products and solutions that are made up of data from numerous databases or available through a variety of different distribution channels, it becomes a challenge to offer customers a journey which represents that best experience for them. This requires access to data from many different systems to represent products and services, while the customer journey traverses many different channels that are both physical and digital.

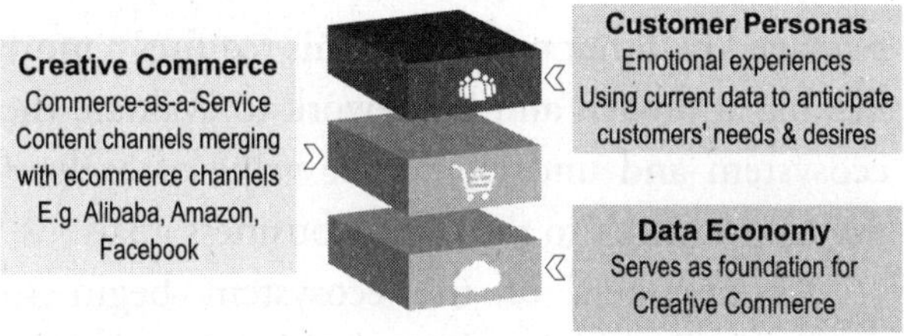


To understand the customer journey through a variety of different systems and channels and the products and services that are relevant to their purchasing history and interests requires access to data throughout the ecosystem.

Throughout distributed eCommerce ecosystems, the combination of data about the customer, location, channel, purchases, products, and services interest is required to improve the experience for the customer and revenue for suppliers. The data is owned by a variety of different entities throughout the ecosystem, which is why a CDEO needs to understand the data and its flows to support the business models.

As customer journeys become more complex, and cross into brick-and-mortar, and participate in a variety of different immersive entertainment mediums, the numbers of members in the ecosystem increase with a greater variety of data points. Most of the data is contained in systems managed by other members. This requires a more flexible approach and framework to evaluate the ecosystem and understand the value of each of the components to the overall business goals.

As members of the ecosystem begin to engage in the marketplace, decisions need to be made on the type of models to utilise the just-in-time access to the data for decision making at the edge of the network or through traditional e-commerce sites. The roles that each of the members will play in the data exchange will differ. Some will be focused on providing transparency in a closed channel, while others will provide snapshots of behaviours. Collecting data without intention or purpose, is costly and ineffective. There needs to be a framework to analyse the data economy, and a plan to capitalise on the use of the data. The framework shown encapsulated several approaches that a CDEO might take to explore different business models and options for data usage. Business goals will drive the overall strategy.

***

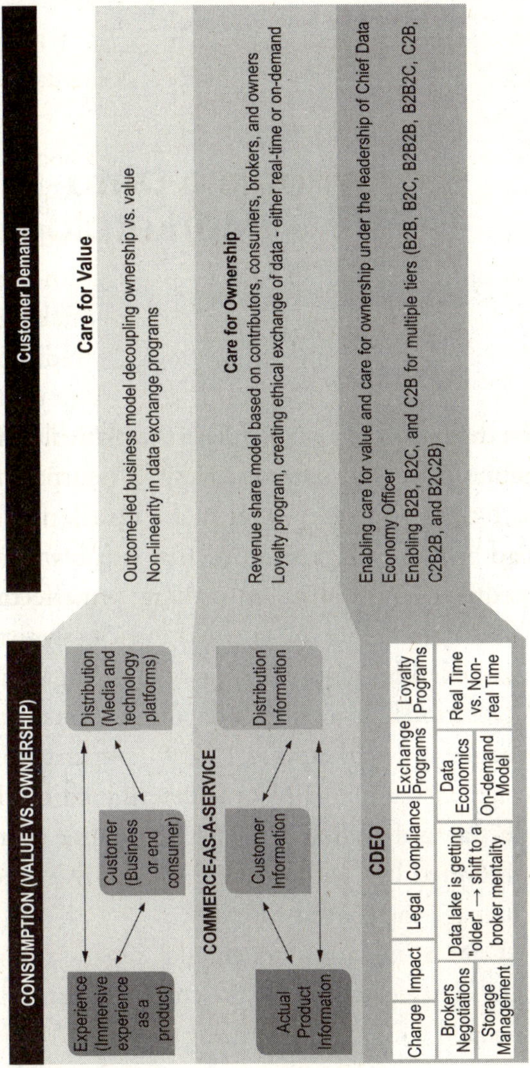
CONSUMPTION (VALUE VS. OWNERSHIP)
Customer Demand
Experience (Immersive experience as a product)
Customer (Business or end consumer)
Distribution (Media and technology platforms)
Care for Value
Outcome-led business model decoupling ownership vs. value
Non-linearity in data exchange programs
COMMERCE-AS-A-SERVICE
Actual Product Information
Customer Information
Distribution Information
Care for Ownership
Revenue share model based on contributors, consumers, brokers, and owners
Loyalty program, creating ethical exchange of data - either real-time or on-demand
CDEO
Change
Impact
Legal
Compliance
Exchange Programs
Loyalty Programs
Brokers Negotiations
Storage Management
Data lake is getting "older" → shift to a broker mentality
Data Economics
On-demand Model
Real Time vs. Non-real Time
Enabling care for value and care for ownership under the leadership of Chief Data Economy Officer
Enabling B2B, B2C, and C2B for multiple tiers (B2B, B2C, B2B2B, B2B2C, C2B, C2B2B, and B2C2B)

Chapter 5

# What Is a Data-Led Marketplace?

The definition of a marketplace is a platform that enables price and data discovery. It is driven by the buyers and sellers that make up the multi-sided market. Organisations that are Data-Led are driven by a decision-making process that utilises data before an organisation can become Data Led. This requires an understanding of the organisational data and the data that is accessible through a marketplace. How organisations engage with a marketplace is determined by the 'role' they are playing in the data economy, which was covered in Chapter 3, and the CDEO needs to manage the process carefully.

Data is an asset, much like organisational financial assets, and there are costs and liabilities associated with storing or using the data. A CFO manages the financial flows and assets within an organisation by carefully working with the executives across the organisation, likewise, the CDEO needs to manage data across the whole enterprise. The tasks of collecting, cleansing, storing, using and sharing the data requires the collective effort to create economic value and improve customer service .

**Data Led versus Data Driven**

There is a difference between Data Led and Data Driven. In a Data Driven ecosystem, the data quickly drives the decision making without human intervention based on what may just be a snapshot of data. Data Led organisations use data as just a component of the decision process, instead of blindly allowing a limited data set to drive the decisions. An example of this could be a self-driving car, a human in the driver's seat could override the car self-driving control to prevent a potential collision or an accident.

In a Data Led Marketplace, the subcomponents of each process within an organisation will participate in the marketplace based on a set of rules specific to the entity as well as the subcomponent. The ecosystems around a Data

Led Marketplace can be complex, as are the data rules that are applied. This is where the CDEO plays a critical role, which is above and beyond the cognitive data driven process. There needs to be a well-defined and purposeful effort to understand the data in the same way that a CFO understands the financials of an organisation, the cash flows, business models and intended value generation for every dollar spent within an organisation. It is not a static image; it is about the return on investment for every business process in the organisation.

The sub-components within the entities that make up an ecosystem and engage with the marketplace, will contribute or access data according to different levels of permissions. In addition, for each sub-component of a process there are different rules associated with the data use or accessibility.

For example, an asset management application for construction equipment may track the geographic location of equipment to automate a type of geofencing which limits the unauthorised use outside of the contracted area. This information may not be available to other systems that do not have a need to access the inventory and its geographic coordinates.

Innovative companies that are driving services through their platforms, need to understand the role that their platforms are playing in the data economy as discussed in Chapter 3 before they can create a strategy. The next step is to understand the many vectors of the data needed to support the business requirements and acquire the appropriate data within the ecosystem. Some models only require a derived insight while others require access to the extensive amounts of data.

## USE CASES

### 1) Artemis – AgTech Company

The First Industrial Revolution dramatically transformed the labour force when 90 per cent of the American population had been focused on farming and workers were transitioning to factories, redefining lifestyles, and product manufacturing. The number of farms has continued to decline. According to Time Inc, the United States has lost many farms in the past decade and debt is at an all-time high while more than half of farmers have been operating at a loss since 2013.

Artemis is a young AgTech company founded in 2015, that enables indoor growers to achieve greater efficiencies using their own data when fed into the world-class Cultivation Management Platform.

Part of their company mission, 'Data informs us, but people inspire us', encapsulates the company's values. They are an example of a revolutionary Industry 4.0 company that intimately understands their customers' journey and pain points, which enables them to focus on customer goals and not just technology. In general, technology can be expensive, and alone it will not achieve customer goals.

Allison Kopf, the founder and CEO of Artemis, has built an intelligent SaaS platform that enables indoor growers to empower a more efficient labour force while utilising the data and technology to grow revenues and create strategies for higher yields. In her TEDx talk, she walks through several examples that demonstrate why technology and automation alone do not achieve the best financial outcomes for growers. It is the holistic customer centric approach to problem solving and the use of data to increase yields and create strategies to achieve goals that have enabled the success of the company and its customers.

The ability to improve outcomes in an indoor closed environment, by utilising data, is one of the things that drove Allison to build Artemis.

Traditional outdoor growers are still in the risk-triage space with many uncontrollable factors. The company was founded with the goal of offering a workflow automation software platform for the farmers and their teams to pull all the information in one place so that they get a complete picture and layer the analytics and lenses to enable improved decision making and outcomes.

The platform manages everything from start to finish, including the raw materials, seeds, plants, irrigation, climate control, temperature, CO2, pH balance, irrigation, labour, growth time, harvested yield, movements, losses, outputs, nutrient, light levels, historical data, food safety, compliance, and anything else that happens operationally. The platform is built with APIs to pull data from any sensors or IoT devices in addition to offering the ability to enter data manually.

The correlation between growers' data and yields can enable growers to make controlled decisions that improve the performance of crop production. Each growing environment will have many different variables, and the data is analysed by machine learning algorithms within the platform to make recommendations specific to that farmer's environment. Confidentiality of the data is critical, and data is not shared since the learning is a competitive advantage for the farming business.

Indoor agriculture is growing quickly and offers several efficiencies and benefits especially as populations continue to grow. The benefits extend beyond just locating facilities closer to the points of consumption. In the Artemis yearly reports they identify several types of facilities which include Indoor Vertical Farms, Aeroponic Greenhouses, Aquaponic Greenhouses, Container Farms, Hydroponic Greenhouses, Soil-based Greenhouse and In-Home Systems. The startup costs for many of these new facilities can be expensive, yet the ability to control and monitor conditions enables the growers to significantly improve their yields by utilising their data to gain insights and create effective strategies.

Each grower uses their own data in their analysis, which fuels the insights and strategy. The platform utilises Machine Learning and AI to analyse the information pulled through APIs from a variety of sources, including manual entry to different types of sensors. Every grower has different conditions and goals which make the data specific to their environment, the platform has the intelligence to interpret and analyse the data. Since the data, strategies and financials are considered a competitive advantage for the growers, this information is kept confidential.

Today, Artemis is empowering smart growers using data, and tomorrow it is possible that the integration with vendors will enable more powerful insights or automation. There are many benefits to the controlled environment agriculture movement, which is projected to grow to more than $142 billion industry by 2024. They utilise less water and space and can be strategically located closer to the distribution hubs. Indoor farming can be expensive to set up initially but being able to make timely decisions that drive higher yields leads to improved ROIs for the businesses.

**2) IOTAS - Smart Apartment Ecosystems**

IOTAS is an award-winning company in Portland Oregon founded in 2014, that enables connected living with smart apartment ecosystems solutions that automate many aspects of property management. The company founder and CEO, Sce Pike, came up with the idea of building the platform when she realised there was a need to manage the fleet of IoT devices in the home and the data that is created. Her extensive experience in wireless helped her envision a platform that did not just control devices within the walls of a living space, the concept of home was a much bigger experience.

It is not just about saving money or automating repairs before there is significant damage, it is about enhancing the experience of the resident, making the notion of home something that is more than 4 walls and a roof but a home that remembers you and recalls your preferences and settings and follows you from home to your next home.

When she conducted her initial market analysis of the connected home space, she determined that her target market of early adopters was likely to move 11 times before the age of 40. DIY Smart home systems were hard to install and integrate, which made it more challenging and less practical for adoption to take off, especially if people were moving every few couple of years. The catalyst that motivated the move into the space came when a building owner and property manager of a large apartment complex that spanned three city blocks was interested in using technology as a competitive advantage. This created an opportunity to test out the Multi-Family-Home market.

The team began by architecting a solution with 40 devices and end nodes per small apartment and within five days implemented over 4000 devices within the apartment complex. Compared to the average smart home which only uses-10 smart devices, the first implementation had four times the numbers of devices. The uniformity of the rental market floor plan allowed for a solution, where a cookie cutter approach to implementing smart home solutions created economies of scale.

This kicked off an analysis of the real estate industry with an understanding of the competitive advantage for property owners to have complete management through IoT devices. It was clear there was a need for a type of fleet management of IoT devices and the layers of data associated with the devices, the resident, and the property management.

While the hardware is owned by the building owners, IOTAS also creates an application and Smart Home experience on behalf of the resident. The data ownership is complex, the property management has one layer of data and control, while the resident is interested in the use of a different layer of data. There are several tiers of data, for example, a water leak alarm that helps limit the water damage while triggering an automatic repair is valuable to the property management, building owners and shareholders. The concept of home for the residents is made up of the data and not by the boundaries of the walls. The residents utilise the data to power an experience throughout the apartment and building property, yet that experience extends beyond the space enabling a new definition of what makes up the home.

Unlike the early days of mobile devices, where the data was stored on devices where it was limited in its portability and use, the connected home data can utilise a wider scope of data from networked devices to make intelligent decisions on behalf of the resident. This is what enables the use of a collection of memories or other data points that analysed together could identify potential issues like the safety of a family member. The individual data points from each sensor alone may not be capable of identifying an issue, but the combination of data points together with historic data will offer intelligent insights.

For the property management, the automatic

alert of a maintenance issue creates a ticket for repair which will automatically schedule a repair at the right price point and timeframe that works for the residents, property manager and the property owner. In addition, the access can be automated to grant the repair person access to the building, elevator, and apartment at a specific point in time what has been agreed to by all parties.

The platform together with the IOTAS hubs that connect all the end-nodes, are created by IOTAS. The data resides in the cloud and is analysed within the platform. This moves away the idea that each device is owned by an individual or an account. For example, the integration of Alexa enables each resident to have an account at an apartment level where the resident does not have to own each device individually. Once the resident moves, the building manager can wipe down the account and reset all the devices at an account level and not have to operate at an individual device level, making it easier to manage spaces. In addition, the data could travel with the resident as they transition to a new home.

The data ownership aspects associated with the data privacy, data security and data ownership are complex. Partners and customers are very data focused on data compliance, trust, privacy, and safety concerns. The long-term vision for the company is to enable the owners of the data the opportunity to own and monetise their data on a marketplace, where vendors or other sources could pay for access.

The vision is to enable the generators and owners of data to have the option to create passive incomes by granting access to their data. To accomplish this, the journey of the data and the intersection points need to be understood to begin to assess the value of the data. The data ownership needs to be well understood to eliminate any liabilities and is a critical aspect of any negotiations with partners and vendors.

Limiting the access to data is critical for safety reasons as well, which is why an approach of less is more and scrutinising all requests for data access is critical. This is a very demanding aspect of the data management that requires limiting its access and only utilising the minimum amount based on a variety of factors. While IOTAS utilised anonymised data from those that have opted in to share their data for analysis, it is very protective of the privacy of all data.

If the data identifies a risk to the building,

like a leak or a fire, it will automatically trigger an alert and an action, otherwise the data is kept confidential. The owners of the data have the option of deleting data at selected intervals of time. IOTAS acts as both a broker of the data on behalf of its ecosystem and in the future on behalf of the owner of the data which may be the residents, building owners, or the devices.

In the future, the ability to take the data and drive cognitive action becomes a possibility. Data driven cognitive actions without the intervention of humans takes Data Led actions which have human interactions at the executive level. Today, the IOTAS platform performs many Data Driven actions on behalf of the building management, like repair requirements where the service people are contacted automatically and granted access to the building.

While everyone intuitively knows there is value in data, it is not clear if all entities producing data understand the 'industrialisation of data' which requires a much deeper understanding of the vectors of the data and all the intersection points. Many leaders use intuition to judge the value of data, and yet there is an emotional layer on top of the data layer that plays a role when making decisions. In addition to the concept of a Chief Data Economy Officer, SEC believes there is a strong need for a Chief Data Compliance Officer as part of the team to navigate the compliance aspects of capturing, utilising, and storing data.

**3) Equipment Financing & Circular Economy**

The equipment financing space has been transforming for several decades, long before the connected economy and web connectivity began to evolve. Patricia Voorhees, who as a leader in the space first at IBM and later as a General Manager of the Office Equipment at GE Capital, is driving transformation into the connected economy with the use of sensors, IoT devices and data, which is enabling new business models as equipment manufactures transition into services and software businesses.

In the early 1970s, Xerox was the first to transform from equipment sales into leasing and services for a monthly fee. They created a captive finance entity to help finance the equipment, which would make it easier for customers to work with Xerox in a more committed relationship. This enabled Xerox to own the customer relationship and their needs making it more difficult for competitors.

They initiated a service with a monthly base minimum fee per machine with an additional cost per copy model, and all the maintenance, toner, paper, and supplies were bundled into the pricing. The Xerox service people had to go in each month to read the meters and determine the usage to send out the monthly bills.

As other manufacturers and distributors of competitive offerings for 'cost-per-copy' models evolved, GE Capital stepped in to finance this business. The model for other manufacturers was slightly different because independent dealers provided the servicing, and they were part of this new service model. The business models for competitors included the business and financial risk associated with the distributors, which GE was financing.

This grew to be a large business for GE with a large volume of low cost per transactions where the monthly payment satisfied the lease payment and the monthly service fees were a passthrough to the distributor that provided the additional services. While the contracts favoured GE Capital because customers needed to pay the monthly fee regardless of the services or condition or the printer, it was clear that customers would not be willing to pay for a copier that was not working.

Mitigating the risk required being able to monitor the service levels and having the opportunity to replace the service providers if they were not functioning properly. There were a lot of issues with the reconciliation of the data, for example understanding where the copiers were physically located within a large enterprise was an issue at the end of a lease. The Xerox model has become the norm in the copier and office equipment space and today copiers still have the highest penetration of leased office equipment because of Xerox's early innovation in the space.

Today in the connected world, the ability to locate equipment and the state and level of utilisation of equipment can be captured by the sensors in the device and sent automatically. In addition, the utilised data can also be used by the sales team to recommend upgrades or new types of solutions or services. This data also enables the understanding of 'risk' especially as new models begin to move towards a no base minimum fee, called a hell or high-water fee.

There are risks in the underlying underwriting

of the asset value and the associated services that can be better understood through the data. Establishing flex-contracts where the customers contract services within ranges so that the pricing, usage, and services are understood upfront is driven through data. Financing managed services contracts requires understanding the credit risk and asset underwriting risk in addition to the customer utilisation risk. The data about the asset, usage, customer credit provides the insights to establish the parameters for the flex-contract that will reduce the financial risks. These multifaceted models present more forms of risk than a traditional financing option.

Flexing down requires a clear understanding of the risk, pricing and underwriting and flexing up requires being able to trigger the required level of services to satisfy the customer needs. The end-to-end data that is available for the asset value, the customer credit, equipment usage and servicing is now available to feed analytics that are available to the companies that are financing equipment so they can properly price the risk for each specific customer environment.

Equipment financing today is serviced by the Capital Markets utilising Asset Based Securitization

(ABS) deals that are driven by the visibility offered by the data lens that enables transparency around every detail about the asset, including the location which was a challenge in the pre-connected economy.

The Capital Markets have eligibility criteria and will determine the size of a risk hedge calculated from the data. As the Capital Markets are becoming more sophisticated in the utilisation of equipment data that is transmitted in real-time to determine what assets are eligible for securitisations. In the long-term, manufacturing companies that do not offer this level of data will not be able to secure the funding.

One of the biggest issues with most assets is underutilisation. For example, in the construction space there could be equipment that is only utilised at 30 per cent but renting the equipment when needed can be very costly. Equipment Share is a company that has come into the space with a new business model offering some rental equipment, while also offering a marketplace for equipment owners to monetise their own underutilised equipment. They utilise sensors, IoT, telematics and even geo-fencing to manage the use and location of the equipment. The parameters are set by the equipment owner to manage the utilisation and location of the equipment and the renter will not be able to use the equipment outside of the agreed scope because it will not work.

**4) A-Track-Tek**

Here is another company doing something similar in the fork-lift space. This model is relevant to the Circular Economy since it reduced waste.

A company in the healthcare space, Cohealo, that understood early on how healthcare costs are rising, and yet expensive operating room equipment has 30 per cent or less utilisation. They developed a data driven solution that enabled tracking the assets, location and utilisation making it possible to leverage the use of that equipment by managing the logistics of schedule or moving the equipment within the healthcare network when needed. Healthcare is typically focused on operation expenses versus capital expenses, but the COVID19 crisis changed the focus as elective surgeries and other non-COVID19 related healthcare services were halted which dramatically affected the cash flow.

New COVID requirements also required a better understanding of equipment inventory and locations to be able to quickly track down needed ventilators and other types of lifesaving equipment. As a result of the new requirements for maximizing utilisation across healthcare systems with a ventilator program, FEMA and the American Healthcare Association awarded Cohelo a contract. This validated the Cohelo business model and sped up the sales cycle for future. Cohelo was recognised as the first healthcare sharing economy solution named both to Fast Company's Most Innovative Companies list and CNBC's Disruptor 50.

### Data Led Marketplace Framework

The best way to visualise the data and its value in an ecosystem is to utilise the Data Led Marketplace Framework to define the characteristics of the data that are specific to that market and industry. Some of the characteristics that need to be analysed include the Volume, Variety, Velocity, Value and Veracity, which may have different values across industries. While some industries may have higher volumes of data, the variety of the data may be more limited. Time may decrease the value of certain types of data, for example, shopper intent data may only be valid for a short period of time for low-cost items that require limited analysis by the consumer.

Volume, velocity, variety, and veracity were the initial parameters used to describe the characteristics of big data. Eventually value, variability and visualisation were added. This framework goes beyond the short list of former definitions that were used when the concept of Big Data began to evolve.

Originally Volume, Velocity, Variety and Veracity were the original paraments, eventually Value was added to the list. Regions, Regulations, Risk, Culture and Sustainability are also critical attributes that provide critical vectors that need to be understood.

- Volume is growing exponentially because of the internet and connected devices. Not all industries produce high volumes of data, although not all data has the same use case, for example machine learning needs a sufficient level of data to train an AI system.
- Velocity is critical for real-time systems where transactions are reacting to data as quickly as possible. Velocity is correlated to the value of data. When sensor data is driving processes at the edge of networks in real time, speed is critical. Institutional financial traders interested in obtaining trade data at

the fastest possible speeds set up servers co-located at the exchanges. Spread Networks, launched an ultra-low latency speed for high-frequency traders in 2009, which improved roundtrip time from 13.1 milliseconds to 12.98 milliseconds.35 The company, which was founded by Dan Spivey and backed by James Barksdale, spent $300 million on this business which demonstrates the value of velocity of data in some businesses. While speed is critical for internet advertising marketplaces, the value on a per transaction basis is small. On a cumulative basis, the volume for internet advertising is high which is what supports the economics.

- Variety in the number of data sources has grown with the evolution of the internet, social media and connected devices. Cleaning, storing, accessing, protecting, and interpreting the data has costs, therefore it is extremely critical to treat data as an asset that is properly managed. The liabilities that exist with certain types of data can be more than a company's worth. In the past, companies saw little impact from breaches and after a short period of time the company share prices would rebound and executives would not be penalised. The liabilities associated with different types of data are very different, for example a recent IBM and Ponemon Institute study calculated the cost at $242 per stolen record, and new regulations will increase the potential liabilities.

- Veracity in data is important, especially since data needs to be cleaned and understood before used. For example, IoT devices can produce noise or fail. Campaign engagement and the correlation to customer interest is not as simple as looking at website traffic. There could be other unaccounted influences that influence the outcomes.
- Value is one of the most critical attributes of data, which is difficult to understand. When used effectively, it can generate financial benefits, but some types of data can generate liabilities, if used or stored incorrectly, that can ultimately bankrupt an organisation.
- Region is a variable that changes the rules associated with data. For global organisations lookingtostreamlinemanufacturingoperations, there are efficiencies in understanding regional similarities and differences before rolling out a

global product that does not require separate manufacturing processes in each region.

- Regulations have become more important than ever because the liabilities associated with the inappropriate use or ineffective storage of different types of data can include personal executive liabilities.
- Risk for data has many different vectors. There is the liability of misuse or cyber theft, but there are other issues as well. When data ages, it loses its value. Access to data on a timely basis is also critical. Situations like outages and vendor lock-in can limit an organisation's ability to extract the value of the data.
- Culture is not always thought of as a critical attribute for data, but the environment where data is used is important.
- Sustainability is critical to measure and without data it is difficult to understand corporate social performance and the correlated financial performance.

#### Tenets of Data led Marketplace

A data led marketplace should have a few tenets that are central to the successful implementation with engaged members. These different elements could include Financial Services, Supply Chain Execution, Industry Item Catalog and Resource Optimisation. They consist of the services that make up the ecosystem and produce data that could be utilised by other services to improve efficiencies or create new business opportunities.

Logistics fulfilment and transportation produce data that could be utilised in the supply chain execution. Easy tracking of Demand and Growth is valuable to E-Procurement Services since it offers increased efficiencies in the workflow.

A market ecosystem is made up of numerous processes and entities that generate data throughout the workflow that is of value to the other members of the ecosystem. The marketplace makes it possible for this data to be shared with economic considerations.

**Solutions**

With cloud technologies offering more modular functionality as a service, data should also be available as a service with built-in economics for the connected participants. With the ability to access or offer data throughout a workflow or ecosystem, there needs to be a marketplace with rules, roles, and embedded economics.

Setting up the marketplace requires the understanding and the development of a shared ecosystem. The data strategy needs to incorporate insights as to how the data will be accessed in real-time, seamlessly, and securely at the application level. The revenue streams will be based on the value contribution and the role within the ecosystem.

### Each Industry has Different Characteristics

The characteristics of data vary significantly by industry sector, which is why it is critical to measure against industry metrics to utilise a framework to create effective strategies. The chart below shows examples of industry metrics, which offer a starting point for goal setting. The opportunity to evaluate their position also requires understanding their 'role' in the data economy. The CDEO can evaluate different strategies with different vectors.

In the chart below, there is a weighted value associated with each of the characteristics of data. For example, for the Volume characteristic, for most of the industry sectors it is either High or Medium to High across all the industry sectors shown, yet the speed of the data varies from low to high. Smart Infrastructure with IoT devices and sensors drive real time processes. Fintech can consume data in high speeds for high-speed trading environments or in processing financial payments when a customer is standing at a register, yet there are some fintech applications which include some lending approvals that are less dependent on an immediate response.

Health Sciences will have a much wider variety of data types throughout an organisation and the data will be in different formats than a consumer-packaged goods company or a wholesale distributor.

EXHIBIT 1 | Ten AI Applications Drive Most of the Growth in CPG

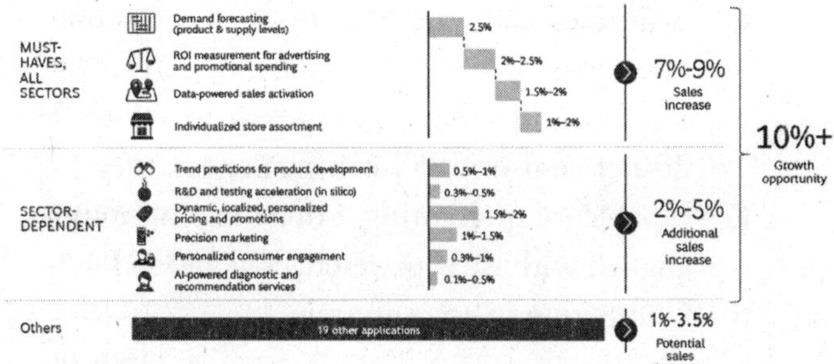


**Source:** BCG analysis.
**Note:** Sales increases correspond to the potential top-line impact of fully implementing a particular application.

**"Must-Haves"**

1. Demand forecasting for existing and new products by SKU and region.
2. ROI measurement for predicting the impact on sales of advertising and promotional spending.
3. Data-powered sales activation for identifying the right retail outlets/points of sale at which to activate the applications and the right set of sales actions to take at the point-of-sale level to maximise market share.
4. Optimised product assortments at the individual store level.
5. Strategic Priorities in the Consumer Goods Industry.
6. Delivering personalised outcomes.
7. Enabling new business models.

a. SAP research reveals that direct-to-consumer sales grew by 34 per cent in 2017, but businesses still have a long way to go. Only 20 per cent of CPG companies say they are capable of presenting offers to consumers aligned with their preferences as needed.

8. Competing in an ecosystem.

The weight of the data attributes will vary by industry and the framework allows an entity to set a strategy for their data with a barometer to set goals, measure performance and evaluate strategies to make decisions. The various vectors that are associated with data differ by industry.

***

Chapter 6

# Finding the Value

Not all data is created equal. The understanding of the potential value of data to an organisation has grown as intangible assets become the most valuable assets for organisations. Yet only ten per cent of data that is gathered is used, and many organisations are unaware of the data that is generated.

The World Economic Forum predicted that by 2020 there would be 44 zettabytes [1] of data, and by 2025 the estimate is that there would be about 463 exabytes of data created each day. In 2013, IBM indicated that 90 per cent of data was created in the past two years, and data growth has accelerated with exponential growth. Enterprises are generating greater volumes or data, without roadmaps to understand, classify, assess, collect, tag, utilise, manage, and govern appropriately.

The work required to extract value from data, creating strategic assets, has been called 'mining' because of the parallels associated with oil. The major difference is that data can be built upon to create additional layers of value. The many facets of data and textures of data types mean that mining is different depending on the company and business processes it supports.

The economic value or strategic importance of data to an organisation cannot be determined if the data cannot be analysed in the context of the business objectives and the role an organisation plays in the use of the data.

The economic benefits to an organisation cannot be extracted without a framework, process, and the appropriate tools. The first step requires an understanding of the types of data that exist within and organisation. There are several ways to categorise and store data, but there are many other critical factors that contribute to the value of data.

1) Inventory: What Categorisations of Data are Relevant?

Understanding what data an organisation owns, gathers, and has access to as well as the different attributes associated with each data type is the first step towards extracting the economic value available from the data. There are costs associated with gathering, sorting, and protecting data, which can make data a liability and less of an asset when it is not understood and managed properly.

According to a study by Splunk, 76 per cent percent of the survey participants agreed that "the organisation that has the most data is going to win." As the Global Datasphere continues to grow at an exponential level, extracting the value and managing the growth of data driven businesses is becoming more complex.

Data governance and data inventories are managed at department levels by the Data Stewards that oversee the data confidentiality, integrity, and

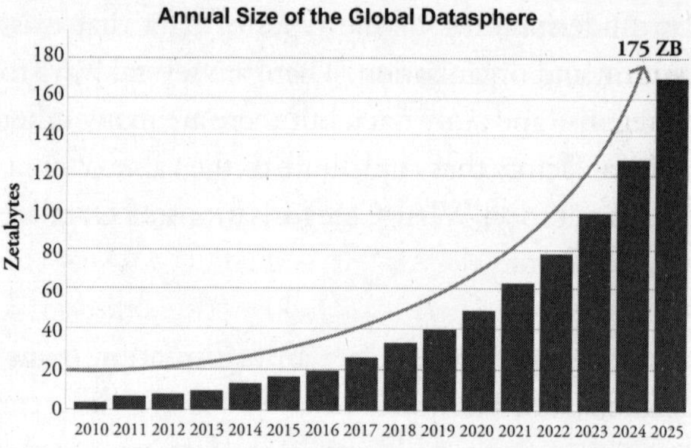


**IDC Datasphere Growth - IDC Report Annual Size**

availability of data sets over the life cycles that apply. It takes more than just categorising data to create value, but it is the critical first step.

There are many ways that Data Assets can be categorised depending on who is responsible for the data and the goals of their department or organisation. We will explore a number of these different approaches, to better understand what is required. Many of these categorisations are independent of each other and only focus on a specific facet of the data.

**A) Security Classifications of Data: Data Assets Protection**

The NIST (National Institute of Standards and Technology) Cyber Security Framework, created by a US Executive Order, defines data as having three core cybersecurity objectives with the acronym CIA. Confidentiality, the C, represents the need to protect data from unauthorised access and disclosure. The I, represents Integrity, which requires the data to be accurate and remain unmodified by bad actors. The Availability, the A, ensures the availability of the data on a timely basis to authorised entities.

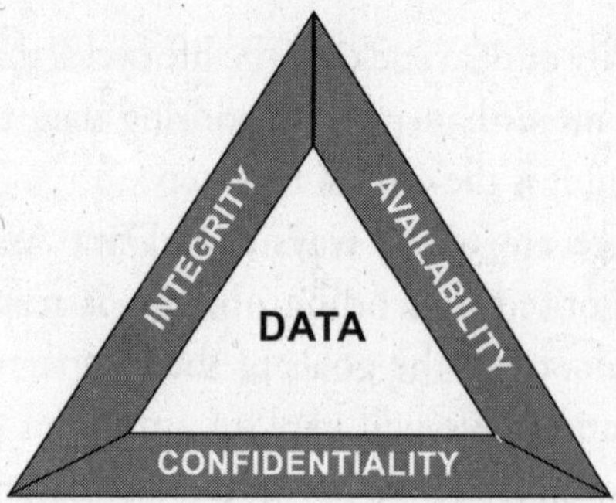


**NIST: The Three Pillars of Information Security**

**B) Access to Data Defined by Classifications**

While 'Availability' is a component of the National Institute of Standards and Technology (NIST) Cyber Security Framework, it is not the same as 'Accessibility' since data access should be limited based on classification and other criteria. It needs to be clear what data should be available to specific entities, partners, suppliers, customers, internal systems, or specific roles within an organisation. Protecting data also requires understanding the classification associated with the data.

**C) Data and Information Security**

NIST defines and evaluates Data and Information Security based on Confidentiality, Integrity, and Availability, known as CIA. The Confidentiality is defined as the blocking unauthorised disclosure. Integrity is compromised when there is unauthorised modification or destruction of information. The Availability of data and information systems is critical and cannot be disrupted by unintentional outages or breaches by hackers.

**D) Levels of Risk**

The risk associated with a breach may have different metrics associated with the severity depending on the effect on the organisation, assets, or individuals. A Low level would only have limited adverse effects. A Moderate level of risk would have serious adverse effects, while a high-risk would have a catastrophic effect on the same entities. There are data classifications that are associated with government and commercial entities that have different sets of criteria. It is not just access that is restricted, the use of the information is also restricted even if the data is anonymised and aggregated.

### Government Classifications

There are different government classifications associated with different countries, but the basic categories range from Top Secret, which is the highest level of security for classified information, to Unclassified, which is declassified or does not have the requirement for a security level classification. A Secret classification would be associated with protecting national security at a critical level while Confidential would be seen as damaging if made public. Sensitive or Restricted would be associated with private content that would have undesirable effects if disclosed. Government classifications can be further defined by subclassifications or by agency specific classifications schemes. Access to government information requires clearance to compartmentalised information at all levels.

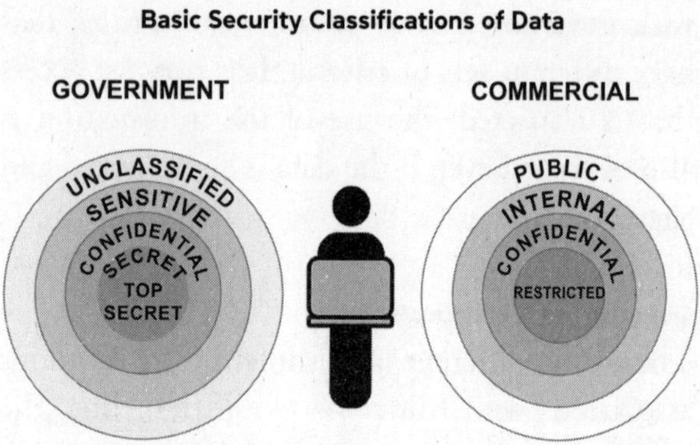

**Commercial Organisation Classifications**

Commercial classifications differ from government classifications specifically because the liabilities and uses of data have different trajectories and values. Government regulations have evolved to protect consumer data and the use of that data, except defining the ownership by individuals and establishing fines for the misuse of personal data. There are many instances where companies have allowed employees to access customer data through unrestricted super user accounts that have created customer confidence concerns and security issues.

A Wired article written as a 'cautionary tale for all companies' described an incident at UBER, where company employees used a feature called 'God View' to track a customer in real time to reveal information about people's personal life or analyse rise data to predict possible indiscretions.

A Twitter hack that reportedly enabled access to over 45 accounts of public figures, including New York Mayor Mike Bloomberg, Bill Gates, and Elon Musk, was because of a 'God View' that provided access to accounts of more than 1,000 people, including some contractors.

Corporate entities define data security and confidentiality rules through a different lens than government agencies. The jurisdiction of the entity and its customer base will govern the rules on data use, possession, custody, or control. The European GDPR and the US Cloud Act are two examples of regulations that define ownership or access to data.

The security levels associated with corporate data sets are defined as Public Data, which is unrestricted, Internal which is accessible to employees, Confidential which is protected with specific access controls, and Restricted, which should be highly protected since it is considered very sensitive or valuable.

#### Data Classification Policy

Corporations need to define the security classification of their data as a first step. Executives and business stakeholders across an organisation should be engaged in the definition and should play a role in defining the risks. The responsibilities associated with protecting the data should be outlined and maintained by each department.

The senior leaders, officers and executives within organisations will incur personal liabilities if data is not handled properly, which

**Restricted and Sensitive Data Requires Discovery and Classification**

Examples:

- Authentication and Access
- Financial Information
- Electronic Protected Health Information - EPHI
- Protected Health Information - PHI and HIPPA
- Export Controlled Materials (Subject to US Export Control Regulations)
- Federal Tax Information - FTI
- Payment Card Information or Primary Account Number
- Personally Identifiable Information - PII
- Personal Data from the European Union (GDPR)
- Government Information
- Confidential IP
- Student Personally Identifiable Education Records

is why creating an effective policy needs to be implemented as a top-down corporate strategy.

**Enabled Access to Internal Information**

Untapped data within organisations remains underutilised because of multiple factors. While data that is collected is not always accessible due to restrictions or the politics of siloed organisations, the bigger issue is the lack of knowledge associated with the utility and value of data.

Most companies are only engaged in the analysis of structured data from siloed systems, but this type of analysis alone does not create new business models.

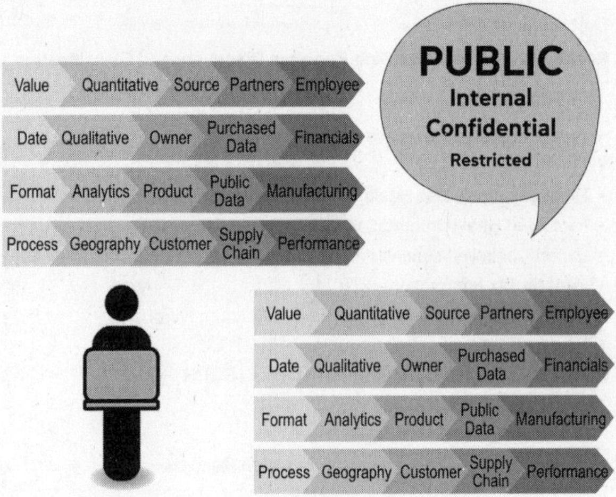


Most organisations cannot accurately access the data available within the entity.

### The Many Vectors of Data in Ecosystems: Value Classifications

The process of understanding what data an organisation possesses begins with understanding all the various classifications of data that exist. Data has many different vectors associated with classification, which makes it challenging to create a dynamic inventory of what an organisation has access to within its organisation.

Within organisations there are data classifications like Strategic, Compliance,

Proprietary and Confidential which identify the value category of the data. The nature of the data, which includes Date, Geography, and Regulations establish a baseline for the use of data. Regulations restrict the use, and over time the value of data decreases.

The science of Data Analytics can offer the ability to take a descriptive, diagnostic, predictive and prescriptive approach towards understanding.

**Qualitative and Quantitative Data**

Unstructured and open data which is not limited, is considered Qualitative Data. The attributes associated with Qualitative Data tend to be sequential (ordinal) sets or finite (nominal) sets of answers that are discrete or continuous.

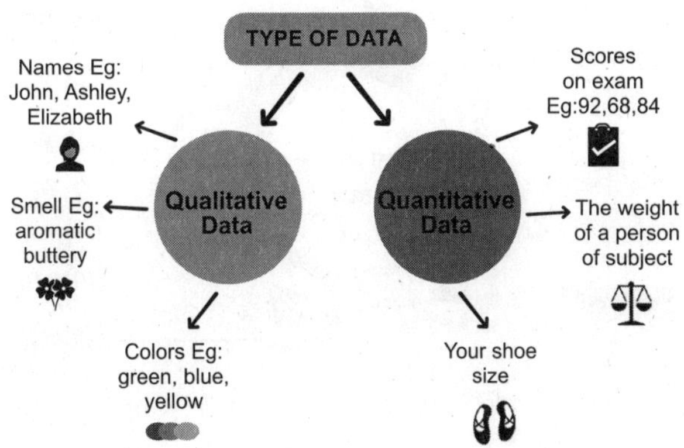

Quantitative data is about discrete, continuous, variable, and categorical data.

#### Data Format

There are many formats and types associated with data. It can be structures, unstructured and semi-unstructured. Volume, variety, velocity, and veracity are the 'four V's' that represent the qualities associated with big data, although value is the fifth V that needs to be considered. The value of the data over time decreases but the opportunities to power new processes or services increases as connected edge computing and IoT grow throughout ecosystems.

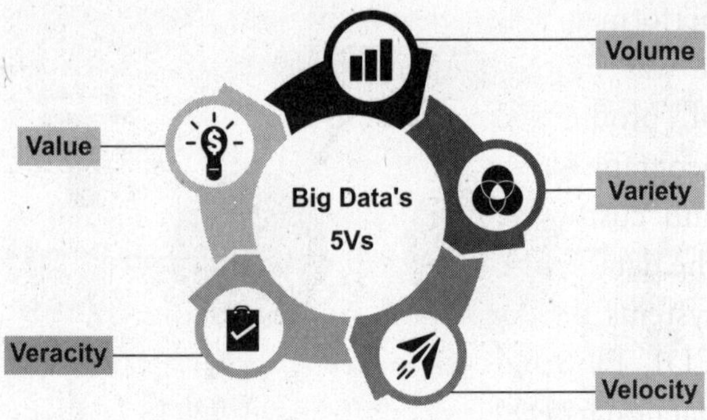

**THE BIG BANG OF DATA**

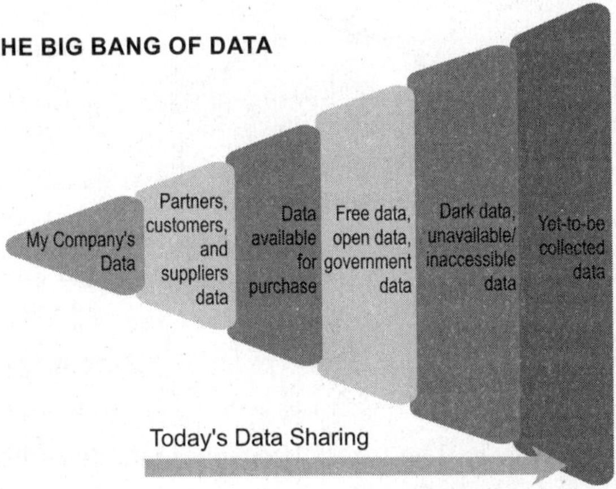


### Data Sources

There are many sources of data within an enterprise. There is confidential information about the employees, financials, processes, customers, partners, suppliers, products, and performance of an organisation. Traditionally, it was more difficult to capture the journeys of products and customers across different geographies, or different systems. As products and customers cross networks and ecosystems, the data remains trapped in the individual siloed systems that own each segment of the journey. EDI, Electronic Data Exchange, has facilitated data exchange between organisations to facilitate transactions.

Customer Data and Product Data is often represented differently in each of the siloed systems, making it challenging to capture full journeys and provide edge solutions that can be triggered to provide improved services. Internet of Things devices, telematics, electronic logging devices, sensors and small embedded computing devices can capture and generate data while also providing powerful calculations at the edge.

**Connected Enterprises: Data Shared through Partnerships**

The internet has introduced connectivity between entities and customers that has generated high levels of big data. In addition, the growth in public data from government agencies, international agencies, external sources, satellites, and partners makes it possible to connect data and capture the intercessions for more insights.

Data sharing in a secure and timely way is often difficult, yet while the technical aspects of data sharing can be challenging, it is the business architecture that defines the value. The data partnerships are built by negotiating and traversing across divisions, silos, and companies to create new opportunities that is the most critical. This architecture has many layers and if the business architecture is not well understood, the value will not continue to grow.

A new type of partnership evolves from the ecosystems which may be providing a service with multiple vendors focused on different aspects. As connected technology and the Internet of Things expands within multiparter ecosystems generating more data, the economics must be defined. The ecosystems cannot evolve and transform without building out the economic layer together with the partners. Hence, the role of Chief Data Economy Officer gets so critical.

The role of the Chief Data Economy Officer is different from other members of the team that work with the data because they are not constrained by the boundaries of systems and organisations. They are empowered to engage with the stakeholders to create a shared value proposition that will benefit each of the members.

### Data Richness & Vectorisation: Data Production, Data Quality, and Data Market

Understanding all the different facets of value associated with data and how that translates into the creation of business opportunities that benefit all the participants in an ecosystem is a critical task for data led digital transformation. This is where many attempts to create new ecosystems have failed, and why it is critical for all members of an ecosystem to understand the value to their business and the requirements for success. This requires a different approach from the traditional agile or business analyst approach of requirements gathering.

There are far more layers that go into creating a successful ecosystem which traverses the technology requirements, the network, the data richness, the use case, the regulatory data requirements, the data ownerships, the economics of the data and the overall expectations of the ecosystem as well as each of the members. The data economics go beyond a simple Software-as-a-Service or some simple subscription service offering.

New business models that expand beyond traditional boundaries and capture or process data at the edge of a network enabled through partnerships require a different approach to engage partners within the ecosystem before architecting the technology layers. Setting expectations at the beginning and tracking the success enables each partner to participate with an understanding of the value their business will gain. This also enables all parties to evaluate what data is critical to achieve the expected goals. Data has become so valuable, that it can also be a liability when shared and used incorrectly. Some members of an ecosystem may not understand the value or their role in an ecosystem and will later pull out, limiting the scope to achieve the goals agreed to throughout the ecosystem.

The definition of the role that is played within a digital economy is a critical first step in negotiating agreements and building partnerships. Some members of the ecosystem will contribute while others create the platform that connects the partners and the data. Each partner in the ecosystem needs to define their goals and how they will engage to create value.

### Setting Expectations

The Data Economy Pyramid is a starting point for setting expectations internally and with the partners in an ecosystem. Each partner needs to define what their intentions and expectations are early in the process. For example, the Data Producer needs to understand what they are contributing and how the data will be captured and stored. It is also important to define what is critical to achieving the specified goals. While there may be many different types of data that can be gathered throughout the ecosystem, it is not economical to capture every data point when they are not needed and could create liabilities. The Platform Owners have different business objectives than those of the Data Aggregators.

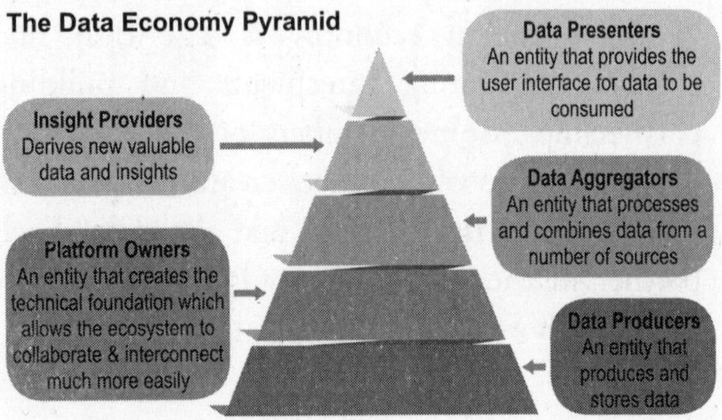

The different roles are defined as follows:

- Insight Providers only acquire the data and provide insights which are contributed to the community.
- Platform Owners build and support the underlying connected infrastructure to collect the data. In addition to contributing to the data, Platform Owners also utilise the data.
- Data Presenters enable the visualisation of the data and consumption of the analysis.
- Data Aggregators take data from a variety of different sources to create insights from intersecting data sets to gain additional dimensions beyond the original dataset.
- Data Producers is any entity that produces and stores the data, taking into consideration the regulatory requirements for the proper governance of the data.
- Consumers of Data contribute value through revenue, and every role consumes some data in addition to contributing to the ecosystem.

### The Framework

Utilising a framework to work through a process helps an organisation to determine the value of the data within the ecosystem. Some organisations will complete the analysis and process in house and others will engage a consulting organisation. Regardless of the makeup of the team, the first step is about understanding the data, the next step requires working through the customer journey which will vary based on the role within the data economy pyramid. The Decision Tree Diagram helps to define some of the dimensions associated with the role in the data economy, while the KPI stage helps define the goals for success for each of the partners and the entire ecosystem.

The framework enables a CDEO to work through a process that enables a richer and deeper understanding of all the different vectors associated with data and the many flavors of the consumers of data. Understanding the customer journeys in combination with all the different vectors of data requires a discipline to work through and extract the value from the data available within an organisation or ecosystem. There are many forms of data that are generated within organisations, but not all data has value and strategy is critical to the creation of the strategy.

### The Chief Data Economy Officer Mindmap

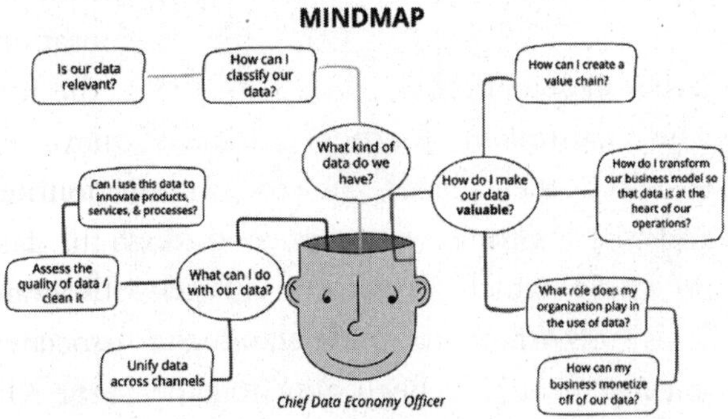


The Chief Data Economy Officer has a critical job laying out the groundwork to understand the data and determine what is relevant to enable the creation of new products and services that are fueled through a connected ecosystem. The first step requires taking inventory of the data that is available and classifying it to understand what data is relevant. There must be a solid general understanding of the business to create a roadmap for new products, services, or processes. Collaboration is an important part of this journey for innovation in connected ecosystems. If the whole ecosystem is not engaged, the plan will not succeed in the long term. A successful transformation will require engaging members of different business units, disciplines, and organisations.

### Customer Journey Map

The Customer Journey Map is used to visualise the phases of the transformation and the customer experience throughout the points in which customers engage with data. It is important to understand the customer journey from the beginning together with the organisational journey, the customer needs, potential opportunities together with the ideas and solutions. The transformation throughout each phase has an emotional curve associated with the value and benefits that are generated by the data in each phase.

The value of this phase of the framework is in enabling an exercise to gain an understanding of how the customer needs and the organisational journey come together to provide the rise in value for the data economy. There are many touch points that define the facets of the journey, while it may look simplistic, it is important to work through the touchpoints to understand how they intersect with opportunities and solutions.©

## CUSTOMER JOURNEY MAP

| PHASES | BEFORE DATA USAGE | DURING DATA USAGE | AFTER DATA USAGE |
|---|---|---|---|
| ORGANIZATION JOURNEY | Data not stored properly; not ensuring quality of data; data not centralised; may not be monetising data | Becomes aware of data; classifies data appropriately; cleans data/data farming: defines organisation's role in data usage | Has data maturity and understanding; Has a data strategy; functioning in data economy |
| CUSTOMER NEEDS | Not discovered yet | Transparency/visibility of data Establish trust, security Fair value | Possesses ability to make better decisions Long-term relationship with org. established |
| EMOTIONAL CURVE | 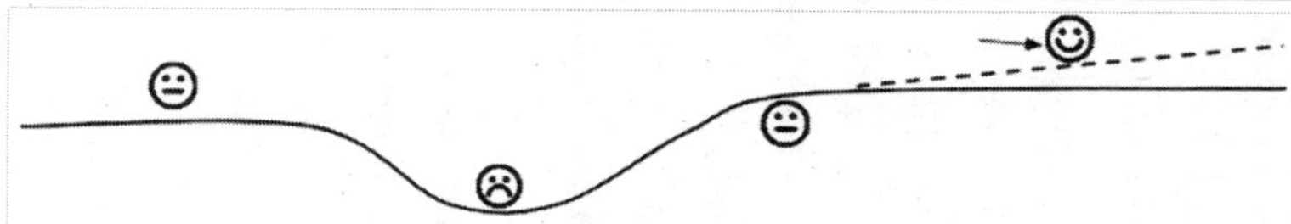 | | |
| POTENTIAL OPPORTUNITIES | Reporting | Predictions Advanced insights | Data economy |
| IDEAS & SOLUTIONS | Intuitive decision making Historic data analyses | New business model & new revenue model - big bets | Networked ecosystem with partners Value proposition |

### Decision Tree Diagram

Data is complex and requires a full understanding of all the layers and the components within each layer. The Decision Tree is a classification tool used to work thorough decision analysis and identify these facets and the implications of the components. It identifies the processes and the decision points. Each of the components has several different subcomponents that need to be thought through. The CDEO can utilise the Decision Tree to evaluate and set operational expectations with the members and partners.

### Key Performance Indicators

Success will be defined by the metrics selected, and they will vary by ecosystem. While some ecosystems will be focused on enhanced services and speed, other ecosystems will be built around by revenue generation. The defined goals may also differ by partners based on their defined roles within the ecosystem, some may want to grow their customer base, while others may want to increase services to an existing set of customers.

The KPIs need to be defined in the beginning so that both the ecosystems and each partner can measure and track expectations. There are far too many dimensions that need to be tracked throughout the ecosystem, and some of the goals may pose conflicts.

One company may want complete visibility, while another company may want to keep some aspects of the information confidential for security reasons. Gaining agreement early in the process enables all partners to align their goals and avoid potential conflicts that would impact the overall success.

#### Required Shift in Organisational Structures

The introduction of a CDEO within an enterprise requires a level of support and collaboration which crosses traditional boundaries within organisations. This is accomplished by the creation of a Data Economy Council where all executives carry some level of responsibility for understanding and driving the growth of the data economy. There is an organisational requirement for communications, cooperation and innovation driven by every member of the management committee that is part of the Data Economy Council.

The chair of the organisation can be rotated on a periodic basis so that every member of the council can drive change and take on the ownership required for success. This makes it difficult for anyone to block the success, since the rotation will eventually put every member in the position of driving collaboration. The organisation cannot succeed if the members of the Data Economy Council do not feel the need to lead or engage.

## DATA LED DIGITAL TRANSFORMATION EXAMPLES

### 1) Heavy Equipment Manufacturing

A heavy equipment manufacturer made the decision to digital transform their organisation from a product company into a solutions company. To accomplish this goal, they made the decision that every product should be intelligent and should capture relevant data. They partnered with leading consulting organisations to help them map out the transition in a way that would create value for customers and members of the ecosystem, while also creating the opportunity to monetise the data that was captured. In addition, the data captured would also help farmers focus on 'smart farming' through their connected farms to improve crop production with higher yields or improved quality. The platform could gather real time statistics with visibility over several years to improve predictability.

They decided that to achieve their goals they needed to engage the organisations that made up the core ecosystem for farming in a town in the Midwest, including the Department of Agriculture, the Chamber of Commerce, and a specialty supplier.

One of the strategic partners was a financial services firm that wanted to increase their digital footprint with the farmers in the rural areas while also providing added value services. The partner contributors and partners that are engaged with the platform wanted to use the data on the platform to plan for the year. There was an interest, by suppliers, in getting insights on the performance and activities associated with 'Organic Farms' versus 'Non-Organic Farms'. Many of the farmers are members of cooperatives today and could benefit from pooled insights that could be obtained on the platform.

A vendor, for example a fertiliser supplier, could gain visibility on how they could provide value to the farmers throughout the lifecycle of each season. If partners didn't want to actively participate on the platform by providing their data, then they would have to pay for the data they would consume.

The data economy concept at the equipment manufacturer started with the idea that all members would be both producers and consumers of the data. Data contributed to the platform is anonymised and all participants gain value from the data.

The leader of customer experience, within the Supply Chain and Logistics Manufacturing Group, launched a data platform where electrochemical sensors on the farming equipment could measure the soil properties. The information captured could be fed into the platform where it could be combined with additional data, including weather and GPS, that could be utilised to predict the potential outcomes for the following season's planting patterns. The platform powers a transition from selling units of equipment or materials to a 'farm-management system'. Participants benefit from the ability to focus on 'smart-farming' through their 'connected farms'.

The financial services firm came on board to obtain the data to gain market share, and due to the politics around privacy it was agreed that equipment manufacturers would be involved in the outreach on behalf of a financial services firm to protect the appropriate use of the data.

This manufacturer was the first mover to engage in digital transformation. The industry had not moved quickly towards the use of sensors, telematics, connectivity, and the Internet-of-things, yet a heavy equipment competitor quickly followed and began to partner with Siemens, Lafarge and Uptake, a data analytics firm to gain valuable data.

**2) Electronics Company and Hotel Chain Partner for Customized or Enhanced Services**

Every time a customer walks into any hotels that are part of this specific national hotel chain, their experience is customised to offer suggestions based on the choices the customer made in the past, or restaurants and hotel chains. Returning customers will be welcomed and targeted special offers and discounts will be offered to the customer.

If a customer walks into an elevator that is part of the hotel chain after checking in, and they are alone on the elevator, they will be offered some activity suggestions they may enjoy within the complex based on what they may have experienced in the past. Voice analytics along with the sensors will determine if the customer is on the elevator and if they are alone, before offering recommendations.

The customisation is enabled by sensors and access points provided by companies like Aruba or Arrowhive, which are capable of processing analytics on the edge in real time based on the data captured from the environment.

Access points on that edge are devices capable of running analytics in real time to check if the customer is new and they will have a different set of targeted recommendations generated for the existing customer. If there are other people in the elevator which can be detected through audio or vibrations on the elevator, the personalised audio marketing pitch on the elevator will stop.

**3) E-Tailoring at Large Retail Store**

A large retail department store offered a programme where customers could be sent several dresses on a periodic basis, and the customer had the opportunity to return the clothes they disliked. The customer choices are fed into their profile and based on what is returned, he e-tailoring profile is customised to improve the selection for the next shipment. The customer benefits from not having to spend time shopping or selecting new items, and the friction around the shopping experience is reduced. The customised experience creates customer loyalty, while increasing the sales opportunity for each customer.

**4) Transportation**

A large metropolitan city transit authority embraced Industry 4.0 by utilising sensors embedded into the buses to improve logistics, enhance performance, improve fuel utilisation, and reduce maintenance costs. A supplier of engines and telematics provided 'connected diagnostics' along with other data that was made available on the cloud. This infrastructure enabled scheduling and maintaining the buses on a timely basis and not just based on the number of miles that had been driven, therefore making the maintenance most efficient and cost effective.

Not all drivers and routes are the same, which is why basing repair on miles alone is not efficient. The city transit authority decided to move forward with the servitisation of the new platform and began to create relationships with companies that were relevant to the ecosystem to participate on the data side.

A third party became the empowered entity within the ecosystem as the data owner, and as the entity grew and gained greater leverage from the control of the data they were challenged by the other members of the ecosystem. The companies that were part of the ecosystem were originally focused on the benefits within their silo and did not immediately see the value of the data from the ecosystem. The data ownership debate eventually slowed down the growth of this opportunity. This is an example of what can happen if there is not a Chief Data Economy Officer in place to work through these types of details in advance, to ensure the momentum continues as all parties engage with an understanding of their role in the data economy from the beginning of the project.

**5) Shipping**

One large shipping company initiated a project that utilised the blockchain to support the entire supply chain ecosystem by providing visibility throughout the entire process. The shipping containerisation process enables the containers to be filled to the maximum based on specific criteria. They created an initiative for 4PL, taking the data and centrally managing, leveraging, and monetising it to make sure that all the parties were in sync.

The benefit of using blockchain is the ability to capture information from several different members of the ecosystem across different entities and silos. Unfortunately, not every member wanted to participate in the ecosystem, only 70 per cent of the members participated.

This eliminated the data richness that was required. There was also a lack of trust between the different members across different geographies making it more of a challenge to capture the end-to-end data required for complete visibility. Without the engagement of all members within the ecosystem, the platform didn't have the level of data richness to track the location of containers across water, ocean, and land.

Some members did not have the data maturity to understand the value of the data. This is an example of why a Chief Data Economy Officer can be extremely valuable in setting the expectations throughout the ecosystem to ensure participation and success, with well understood data economics for each participant.

The restrictions, needs, regulations and expectations can be set upfront by utilising a framework. Without this type of a process and structure, it is extremely difficult to drive change throughout an ecosystem with engagement from all participants. The entities need to determine upfront what their role will be in the ecosystems to drive successful outcomes.

**6) Sustainable Manufacturing**

The creation of sustainable manufacturing businesses, which is part of the circular economy, depends on the use of data.

The manufacturing process and supply chain can be transformed through a data led digital transformation. Benchmarking requires access to data and metrics.

Productivity analysis requires looking at all aspects of the process from the effect of the individuals and biophilic design to drive sustainable manufacturing with APQC benchmark data.

Understanding the requirements for quality assurance and translating them into the setup of the manufacturing plant with sensors throughout the space to maintain consistent temperatures is driven by smart devices on the network that can measure and utilise data.

Quality control and the reduction of returns can be improved by bringing the distributor into the manufacturing environment and developing a close partnership. This reduces the inspections process and returns.

The role of the Chief Data Economy Officer is to understand the data requirements throughout the manufacturing and distribution process to maintain the requirements of the circular economy and engage the partners in the process to meet the requirements throughout the entire process.

***

Chapter 7

# Global Applications:

## Global Initiatives to Fuel Economy with Data

Digital transformation offers the opportunity to evolve and grow as major industries are facing new types of competition. Governments are also recognising that digitisation presents opportunities for economic development, growth, and competitive advantage, if there is a proper framework to develop strategies that work.

Moreover, digital transformation is fuelled by data. While there are many interesting examples of companies that have successfully transformed through data utilisation, it is difficult to understand the economics without peeling back the layers. There are many different vectors associated with that value of data, which is dependent on the industry context, jurisdiction, and the role within the data economy (as described per industry in Chapter 3) for the specific industries. The evolution of networked cognitive and computing systems over the past few decades, has also transformed the types of data that are available, and the value of that data in new distributed processes that can revolutionise business models and customer journeys.

Countries are just beginning to understand the role of data in economies and have introduced legislation and other initiatives to provide guidance, yet most of the guidance falls short of its goal to fuel economic growth, since the focus is on the limits and liabilities associated with data. There are no incentives in these regulatory frameworks to encourage the use of data to transform and grow businesses. Europe is more clearly focused on motivating businesses towards the use of data to drive the digital transformation with its initial development of PSD2 (EU regulations for electronic payment services), which inspired the UK and other regions of the world to develop Open Banking solutions.

### US Data Economy Initiative

Researchers have been exploring the data economy for decades. The Clinton administration directive focused on the analysis of economic implications of internet and electronic commerce, including macroeconomic assessment and the potential implications of information technology. As technology has evolved, the landscape of information creation has also shifted, generating exponentially more data, and pushing powerful networked systems to the edge of networks. As data has grown in value and complexity, local state governments have begun to focus on the legislative framework for data protection and ownership.

### European Data Strategies

On the 19 February 2020, the European Union published a strategy for data- establishing data frameworks to encourage innovation in digital transformation. Data Strategy and Artificial Intelligence are a pillar of the new European Strategy for Data, the goal of which is to drive a level of global competitiveness that will benefit citizens by enabling better healthcare, transportation, public services, energy, financial services and more. The report generated by the European Union states that privately-held data should be used to solve problems, offer better services, and stimulate the economy.

The European Union has taken the lead in establishing regulations around the use of personal data. Currently, it is promoting good practices on Business-to-Government (B2G), through the High-Level Expert Group on Business-to-Government Data Sharing initiative set up in 2018. The new B2G is focused on policy, legal and investment measures across the EU through use of data stewards for data-sharing governance, ethics, and operational tools.

In the recent European Commission Study on data sharing between companies in Europe, only 40 per cent of the surveyed companies reported to engage in the data economy. The European Commission goal is to increase data usage for economic growth and enhanced services, together with increased clarity on the use of data through regulations and directives. The recently published European Commission study defines the various forms that can be taken in the data economy as:

1) Data Monetisation between companies to provision services,
2) Data Marketplaces between trusted intermediaries on a secure platform,
3) Industrial Data Platforms for strategic

collaboration between a restricted group of companies to improve efficiencies, products, or services,

4) Technical Enablers that generate revenue from a solution that utilises data,
5) Open Data Policy companies that offer data for the creation of improved data services.

The data protection regulations and legislation, including the General Data Protection Regulation (GDPR) created in 2016 and the e-Privacy Directive, layout the grown rules for personal data, content, and metadata protection. Two other dimensions of data protection include the data localisation restrictions, which require data to remain and be processed within each member states and the defined barriers to access and transfer.

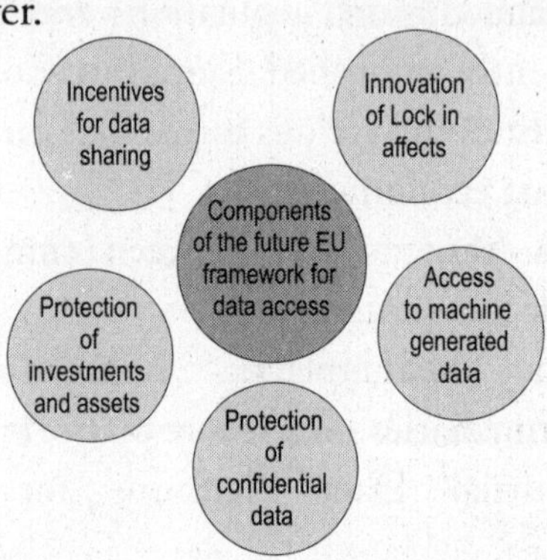

**Components of the future EU "framework" for data access - European Commission**

This extensive legislation created by the EU has generated guidelines across numerous industries including vehicle repair, road safety, smart manufacturing, smart agriculture, smart grids, smart infrastructure, transportation, healthcare, and smart buildings. The data-fuelled growth is critical for the European economy and the report indicates an annual growth rate for the EU Data Market of 9.5 per cent a year, with the possibility of value of $739 billion by 2020.

While the lack of skills, regulations, licensing contracts, and financial resources will continue to limit opportunities. However, the success factors for data-sharing are defined as the availability of a legal framework, understanding of the data demand, trust, partnership, and simplicity. Though the report lists legal uncertainty and ownership rights as a potential roadblock to growth, it is critical that companies have a roadmap that includes a framework defined in this book to help them understand the texture of the various attributes that make up the value of data within the appropriate context.

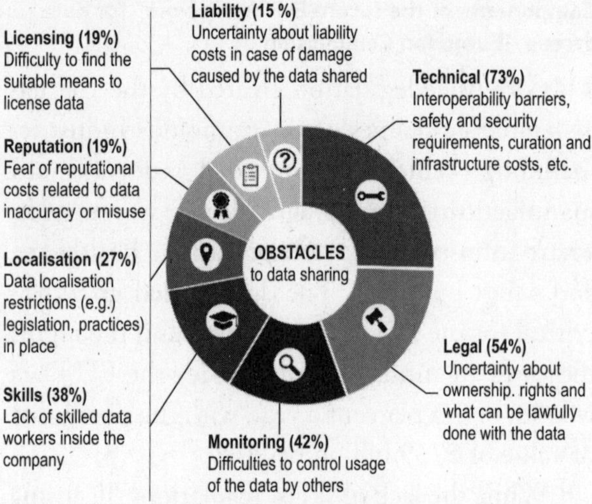


**Identified Obstacles to Data Sharing**

## The United Nations Data Strategy of the Secretary General for Action by Everyone, Everywhere with Insight, Impact, and Integrity 2020-2022

The strategy proposed by the United Nations is established with a purpose to foster outcomes across people, and cultures, partnerships, governance, and the technology environment. The UN did not propose a digital nor innovation strategy. It defined outcomes and data principles based on the UN values for data-driven transformation towards identified priorities and goals.

Data is defined as offering the potential for better support to people and the planet. The expectation within the UN is to identify and deliver "data action portfolios" which engage all levels of the United Nations globally. While this will not focus specifically on the economic growth of economies, it will drive actions towards the defined UN defined priorities.

### Global Initiatives for Data Economy

There have been several initiatives that have been launched around the world to define, create, and grow data economies. The Government of India has been working on multiple bills, including the Personal Data Protection Bill for personal data, Digital Information Security in Healthcare Act, RBI Regulations for Financial Data, and other initiatives are put in place through the government's conducive regulatory ecosystem. The data economy is believed to be critical to the economy and projections of fuelling job growth with the tens of millions of jobs as reported by the McKinsey Global Institute (MGI), yet there are concerns with over regulation.

The IMF report portrays the collection and trading of data as a key input in modern economic production along with traditional metrics of land, capital, labour, and oil, which will drive everything from the future of transportation to healthcare. Yet the development of new industries will extend beyond the traditional digital leaders shown in the Bloomberg and IMF chart below. The IMG report states that economic implications of data flow require more cooperation between regulators within and cross countries.

**Big tech, big value**
**The gains in market value of data-intensive companies have outperformed the average for companies in the S&P 500.**
**(percent)**

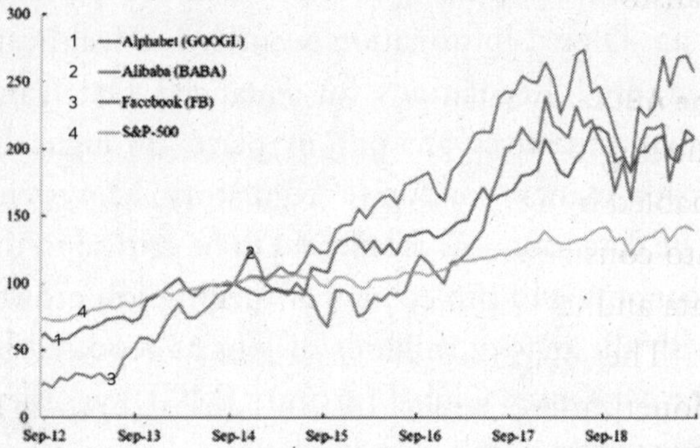


Note: January 2014 = 100.
Source: Bloomberg and IMF staff calculations.

Companies that utilise data to transform will create the next generation of economic value, but this requires frameworks that provide transparency around the economics and motivates organisations and ecosystems to share data to build value and better serve customers. Government Data Economy Frameworks do not fuel growth. Unfortunately, many of the frameworks that have been created by governments do not encourage the sharing of data within ecosystems, because they focus more on the liabilities of data. Therefore, many companies in the European Union, especially small and medium businesses, are still not participating in the Data Economy to transform their businesses.

### The ABCD Monetization Framework

Fuelling economies through use of data is best enabled by a well thought out framework, taking into consideration all the vectors associated with data and its attributes.

The objective of introducing the ABCD Monetization Framework is to offer an approach that goes beyond the work that has been presented, to analyse the data economy with the tools to create fuel growth. Understanding how to utilise the ABCD Monetization Framework, requires understanding the fundamental components of the data economy.

**What ABCD's Role in the Data Economy?**

The data economy pyramid, that was introduced earlier in the book, identifies the different roles that companies can play, together with metrics to assess and score the value creation. Companies can play more than one role. What is more important is how the value is extracted in each of these roles that a company is actively engaged in.

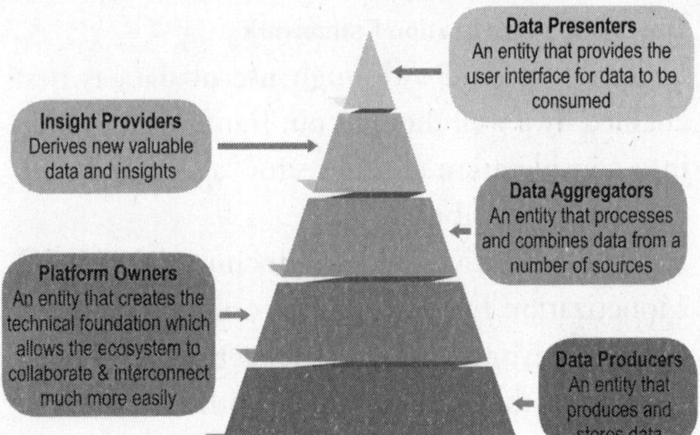

### How is the Data Economy Utilised and Monetised?

There have been many reports and studies that have generated discussion around the data economy, yet the regulatory restrictions do not increase the growth in data usage by private organisations. The recent IMF Report on The Economic and Implications of Data, encourages the creation of policy frameworks for the increasingly complex global data economy, while warning that global cooperation is needed to avoid the fragmentation that comes from borders that limit access. Global Data Markets, including trade and finance, are fueled by cross-border data activity and require international levels of cooperation.

The context and framing of a data economy requires a different approach that is separate from the regulations that constraints on the use of data within jurisdictions.

The IMF reports that data has three economic characteristics that create important challenges for public policy: Data is Nonrival which limits incentives for organisations to share, Data involves Externalities which imposes costs on data collection and Data is Partially Excludable and requires protection of sensitive data, especially personal data. These restrictions do not promote the use of data to create new business models and services which improve the standard of living of individuals or fuel the growth of economies.

Organisational decisions around the generation, storage, use, or sharing of data need to be made within the context of business goals within the regulatory guidelines. This is where the use of a framework helps organisations define and value their strategy, to create new business models that extend beyond the siloed systems to provide value to customers across the subject's entire journey. This is how new business models and services will be created.

#### The Creation of Frameworks for Data-as-a-Service

The first step in creating a Framework for Data-as-a-Service requires the identification of all the Service Attributes. As an example, for a manufacturing company that is transformed through data-as-a-service, there would be a need to define the Service Offer Attributes which would include: Operating Model, Offer Structure, Usage Rights, Channels, Availability, Reliability, Pricing, Discounts, Delivery (Assets), Service Contract, Service Start Date, Cancellation and Termination, Cancellation and Termination

Credits, Billing Models and Frequencies, Taxes, Financials, Services Options, Asset Ownership, Contract Renewal Terms and Extensions, Partners and Commissions.

Each of these attributes requires further analysis to understand the options within the attributes that define the qualities and definition of each attribute. For example, the following chart was created for a manufacturing company as a Data-as-a-Service Reference Model:

**The Creation of Frameworks for Solution-as-a-Service**

Moreover, the same manufacturing company could utilise all the relevant attributes from the Data-as-a-Service to then offer a Solution-as-a-Service which would require a different approach, by utilising the consumption model to digitally transform the business. The Consumption Models would include the identification of the rights, pricing, billing, delivery methods and asset ownership. The analysis would include Subscription and Utility through different types of delivery platforms.

The ABCD Monetization Framework offers a process by which to understand and track all the components and benefits that come from

## Solution as a Service Reference Model (V 1.0)

| Consumption Models | Own Upfront | Upgrade & Support Over Time | Subscribe | |
|---|---|---|---|---|
| Offer Structure | Transactional | Upgrade & Support | Service Subscription | SW Subscription |
| | Company Wide Agreement | | | |
| Entitlement/ Rights include one or more of the following.. | Use of a set number of features/ capacity for product lifetime | Must be purchased with Perpetual license: | Use of: | Use of: |
| | | Periodic content, updates, and version upgrades | Negotiated contract | Features/Capacity |
| | | Technical Support | Standardized Service Description | Periodic content, updates and version upgrades |
| | | | | Technical Support |
| Usage Rights | Perpetual | N/A | Term | Term |
| Pricing | ·Fixed | ·Fixed | ·Up front commitments | ·Fixed |
| Billing Model | Up front | Up front | Up front | Up front |
| | One time | One time or Periodic | | One time or Periodic |
| Delivery Method | E-Delivery or physical fulfillment | E-Delivery or physical fulfillment | Remote | E-Delivery or physical fulfillment |
| | | | Time bound monthly deliverables | |
| Asset Ownership | Customer or Partner | Customer or Partner | Customer or Partner | Customer or Partner |

<table>
<tr><th></th><th colspan="3">Utility</th></tr>
<tr><th>SaaS</th><th>SaaS</th><th>XaaS</th><th>Professional Services</th></tr>
<tr><td colspan="4"></td></tr>
<tr><td>Use of:</td><td>Use of:</td><td>Use of:</td><td>Use of:</td></tr>
<tr><td>Features/ Capacity</td><td>Features/ Capacity</td><td>Features/ Capacity as defined by customer-negotiated contract</td><td>Features/ Capacity as defined by customer-negotiated contract</td></tr>
<tr><td>Periodic content, updates and version upgrades</td><td>Periodic content, updates and version upgrades</td><td>Right to use software</td><td>Equipment</td></tr>
<tr><td>Technical Support</td><td>Technical Support</td><td></td><td>Professional Services</td></tr>
<tr><td>Term</td><td>As you go</td><td>Term</td><td>Term</td></tr>
<tr><td>·Fixed</td><td>·Usage</td><td>·Up front commitments</td><td>·Up front commitments</td></tr>
<tr><td>Up front or Post-paid</td><td>Post-paid</td><td>Up front or Post-paid</td><td>Up front or Post-paid</td></tr>
<tr><td>Periodic</td><td>Periodic</td><td>Periodic</td><td>Periodic</td></tr>
<tr><td></td><td></td><td></td><td>Milestone Based</td></tr>
<tr><td rowspan="2">Cloud (Public or Private)</td><td rowspan="2">Cloud (Public or Private)</td><td>Cloud (Public or Private)</td><td>Build – Own – Operate</td></tr>
<tr><td>Build – Integrate - Transfer</td><td>Consulting</td></tr>
<tr><td>Juniper</td><td>·Juniper</td><td>·Customer or Partner</td><td>·Juniper</td></tr>
</table>

the transformation to facilitate economic growth using data, which include:

1) The creation of a monetisable state of the union.
2) The launch of new business models that can offer customer services that are efficient and cost effective.
3) The opportunity to generate new revenue streams from the new business models that are created from the use of data and information.
4) New pricing models based on a variety of metrics or consumption models.
5) The requirement for a new organisational structure as discussed earlier in the book to support the need to drive the business through the economics of the data as an asset.
6) Development of new processes and assets that create value for an organisation including new forms of intellectual property.
7) A greater understanding of the attributes that enable transformation is critical to facilitating the transformation within each industry.

While the data related frameworks have been introduced by various organisations to drive economic growth, they all focus on the regulatory concerns and liabilities governing the use of data.

| | | | | | |
|---|---|---|---|---|---|
| Utility | Utility | Utility | | | |
| SaaS | XaaS | Professional Services | | | |
| | | | | | |
| Juniper (Direct Channel), Partners (Tier-1) and Distis (Tier-2) | Self-Serive (customer can purchase anytime) | | | | |
| Specific to a deal | | | | | |
| Pre-defined scope (for professional services) | Upfront commitments | Volume based | Deliverable Based | Bundled | |
| | | | | | |
| | | | | | |
| Additional attributes required to bill (like usage / metering etc) | Additional attributes required for service delivery (like entitlement check of valid license) | Includes all assets within a configuration | Includes only a top line PID | Requires Version control | Continuous coverages (desired / mandatory) |
| Upon First Usage | | | | | |
| Co-Termination allowed for simplificaton | Special Conditions (like take-over) | | | | |
| | | | | | |

Continued on next page

| Billing Model (includes both amount calculation and frequency) | One time & upfront | Periodic - Upfront at the beginning of service period (like beginning of each month / billing cycle) | Fixed / pre-calculated amount - Periodic (mile stone) | Fixed /pre-calculated - Periodic (at regular intervals) |
|---|---|---|---|---|
| Tax | Same as Bill-To | Determined by physical location of product installed | Determined by physical location of product installed (additional granularity involved - zip, county etc) | Varies by Type of service |
| Invoice Format | Mandatory One Invoice (for both servcies and products) with tax lines | Separate Invoices (for services and products) | Separate invoices for periodic billing | Billing Statement allowed (in lieu of Invoice) |
| Revenue Recognition | 100% Upon Ship Date of product (or upon contract creation) | Pro-rated over a period of time (period of performance -duration of contract) | 100% upon first usage | Pro-rated over a period of time (period of performance -duration of contract, start date being first point of usage) |
| Service Delivery | On-Premise repair services | Repari services at a repair facility | 100% Replacement Services during active contract period | Loaner products during repair of faulty product |
| Asset Ownership | Customer Owned | Company Owned | Build -Operate-Transfer (ownership is transferred after certain time) | |
| Renewal Contract | Renew contract with no changes to T&Cs (simple renewal) | Allow changes to Contract at the time of renewal | Pre-determined Repricing (% uplift) | Not Allowed |
| Contract Renewal Initiation | Juniper Intiated (Sales Rep) | Partner Initiated | Customer Initiated | Auto Renewal (system initiated) |
| Extension | Allowed at the end of contract (grace period) with no additional charges | Allowed at the end of contract (grace period) with additional charges | | |
| Sales Compensation | | | | |
| Partner Payments | | | | |

| | | | | | |
|---|---|---|---|---|---|
| Agreed upon/ calculated - periodic | As determined (post paid) | One time (post paid) | | | |
| Flat rate (for both hardware/software and services) | Exemptions allowed | Exemptions not allowed | | | |
| Specific legal Invoice requirements (like gap less invoce numbering, display of additional content, invoice currency etc) | | | | | |
| Consulting Services ? (how does it happen in consulting services - is it based on invoice date?) | | | | | |
| No loaner products during repair of faulty product | Advance Replacement (customer ships faulty product later) | Consulting Services (deliverables as determined by scope of work) | | | |
| | | | | | |
| Contract Number is same as original | Mandatory new contract number (with reference to original contract) | | | | |
| Quote-to-Contract cycle is required | | | | | |
| | | | | | |
| | | | | | |
| | | | | | |

smart homes and consumer surveillance technologies, the transformation for large Fortune 100 companies is far more complex. Organisations with hundreds of thousands of employees that have large-scale footprints of computing power distributed across data centers, the cloud or in hybrid configurations are much more complex to transform.

Future Tech Enterprise is playing a critical role in helping with these large-scale transformations through its expertise and partnerships with over 700 technology companies. Success requires more than just an understanding of technology; it requires a deep understanding of the customer businesses and their infrastructure to successfully harness the value of the data economy across customer ecosystems.

Large organisations typically have mastered the management of centralised computing power, yet the ability to harness the power of new computational devices at the edge requires a different approach. This is where the transformation is enabling value creation. More data is being generated at the edge of networks than in data centers. Large organisations are devoting greater amounts of their budget on resources to support this transition. The evolution of

IoT devices and distributed devices on the edge of the network are now far more sophisticated and require less energy to process greater amounts of data.

Partners like NVIDIA, enabling powerful computational functionality, like artificial intelligence, and other data driven processes at the edge. NVIDIA's $40 billion acquisition of Arm is one of the largest in chip making history, and represents the opportunity to grow into new markets where they can power a larger market of IoT devices from smartphones to industrial devices.

There is now a growth of new organisations that Bob calls 'Born-on-the-Edge' that are flexible enough to utilise the data that is generated to power new business models. The value of these new organisations is derived from the data and understanding how to utilise the data to power new business opportunities. It is not just the technology and data collection that generates value, it is the ability to harness the value.

This requires a new skill set and resources to understand and apply the business value that is extracted from the data.

The management of the edge creates new pain points as companies must support a new diverse layer of devices that sits above the traditional firewalls, switches, data centers and enterprise systems. This edge is now the first level of difference for most organisations, although there is an increased level of complexity with the expanded number of remote workers being added to the edge after COVID19. The outside circumference of the edge of networks has expanded, which increases the security vulnerabilities.

There has been growth in the diversity of technologies available, including new hardware devices, CPUs, GPUs vendors, in addition to the growth of consulting practices focused on how to manage the edge and data with industry specific focus. It is very important to understand that 'not all data is created equal' and data has the potential to generate different values by industry or use case.

Best practices are based on market industry specific, with different metrics and definitions for success. Some industries are better positioned to take a bigger leap utilising the technology. For example, the opportunities in aerospace and defense could be transformation. The Internet of Military Things (IoMT) and the Battlefield of Things (IoBT) have transformed warfare.

Soldiers have sensing, and computing devices embedded into their combat suites, helmets, and weapons with high-speed networks for edge computing that together with the IoBT create a cohesive fighting force that utilizes data from many different devices in the field to make strategic decisions.

The Total Economic Impact on the use of IoT Connectivity for logistics, transportation and supply chains can be significant, offering efficiencies while reducing costs. This is another area that will greatly benefit from data generated computing at the edge. Companies like Amazon have implemented resilient end-to-end systems that provide complete transparency, enabling reconciliation of inconsistencies, maintenance, contamination, audits, and quality. Today supply chains require complete traceability, tied to devices and organisations will need to invest on the edge. Supply chains and connected suppliers need to be certified and secure.

If you go back a decade ago, most people would not have imagined the level of maturity of devices operating at the edge including devices like drones or automobiles. Looking to the future, change will be continuing to grow exponentially, and the ideas that at one point were futurist are not that far ahead.

The data at the edge will drive the new data economy fueling many new services, but globally there will have to be a better understanding of the regulatory side of data exchange, especially regarding personal data.

**2) Pharmaceutical Industry**

The pharmaceutical industry is a complex and fragmented global 1.25 trillion US dollar market of 2019, and the development of successful drugs is a unique industry. The four largest market categories are the central nervous system, cancer, metabolic and gastrointestinal diseases, and cardiovascular disorders, accounting for slightly more than half the market in terms of value.

The 2019 oncologic pharmaceutical sales were 99.5 billion USD, overtaking the central nervous system as the costliest therapeutic area. Clinical pathways, cancer management programs and the Oncology Care Model add to the complexity of the healthcare ecosystems. As shown in the diagram below of the Oncology Care Model by the Physicians Advocacy Institute's Medicare Quality Payment Program (QPP) Physician

Education Initiative in the United States, data plays a major role in improving the quality, efficiency and effectiveness that utilizes the OCM episode-based payment system, developed by Medicare and Medicaid Innovation. OCM, which was developed by CMS's Center for Medicare and Medicaid Innovation (CMMI),

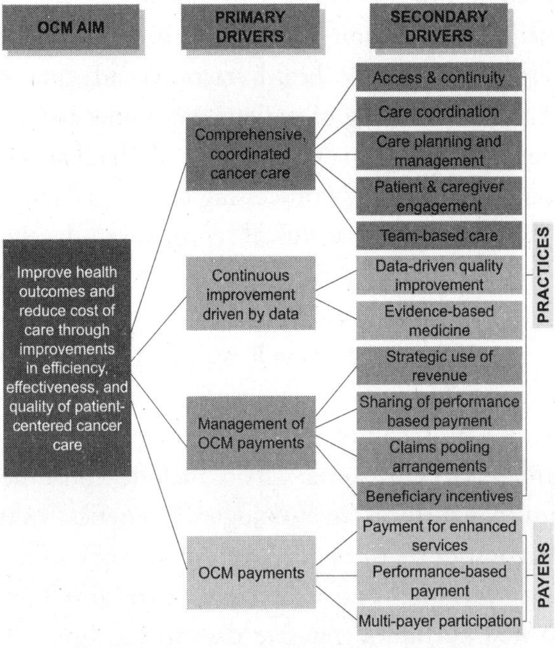


**PAI, Physicians Advocacy Institute and Healthsperien Inspired Health Solutions**

is the highest profile alternative payment model where payments are tied to value creation and performance. Certified electronic health record technology is used (CEHRT) and data is used to drive continuous quality improvement.

The Oncology Care First (OCF) programme is a newly announced programme derived from OCM, which may increase adoption by more healthcare entities to manage a few of the most common forms of cancer. It utilises certified electronic health records and data to enable monitoring of patient symptoms and the identification of high-risk patients. The data also facilitates the timely processing of claims data.

When pharmaceutical companies develop patented therapies for high unmet needs, they can enjoy long periods of healthy profits while competing therapies will suffer a decline in revenue. Many pharmaceutical companies have businesses in complementary healthcare products and services in areas which include consumer health, medical technologies, generics, and diagnostics that provide levels of synergies, data, and learning. The ecosystems that give birth to new therapies generate data that is useful to pharmaceutical companies, especially that which is generated from university research. Today, the ecosystem around data exchange doesn't distribute rewards equitably, and individuals have no control or ability to direct the use of their data for the benefit of developing therapies for some of the most costly and impactful ailments.

A leader in the pharmaceutical industry, Kamayini Kaul, formerly held lead roles involving different facets data at GE Healthcare, Santander and Shire Pharmaceuticals and is currently the Global Head of Data Lakes and Integrations at Bristol-Myers Squibb has an interesting personal perspective.

The global goal of healthcare services and pharma center around bringing lifesaving medication and services to the customer, and as people continue to live longer the need for therapeutics, targeted drugs, life preserving medications and services will increase. At the frontier of the aging population, people are living longer, increasing the likelihood they will be a consumer of these lifesaving and health preserving tools, especially for chronic care. This need is front and center across the whole pharmaceutical and healthcare industry globally, which is driving the focus to find unique drugs and therapeutics for unmet needs where patients have large incidents rates for chronic illnesses.

Today's frontier is the neurological deficits and behavioral therapies. In the 1990s, there was a focus on chronic infectious diseases with vaccines and anti-infectors viral therapies which were focused on the AIDS epidemic, later followed by oncology. The neurological and behavioural fields will be the bigger focus over the next five decades.

Each of the big pharmaceutical companies have been looking at the global trends to determine the highest incidences of declining health where there are unmet needs and choosing which area they would like to focus on. If every company plays to the same set of indications and experiences while targeting the same portion of the value-chain, it will quickly erode the market opportunity for all the players. This approach will not benefit the competitors in that sector of the market, the entire market will only compete on price, and it will not serve the patient population.

While having multiple options will keep the price in check, there is no value creation when 16 different drugs are brought to market for the same need, where every company only competes on price. There are already a large number and variety of different health issues that need to be addressed, having every pharmaceutical company targeting the same exact health issues can be wasteful and will not benefit patients.

This approach detracts resources from focusing on unmet patient needs. For example, oncology is an area of focus for all pharmaceutical companies, and every cancer is different with different mutations, but having every pharmaceutical company targeting the same issues creates challenges. Accessing meaningful sample sizes for clinical trials can be problematic when all the pharmaceutical companies are targeting the same patients.

As a result, different strategies are being selected to go after unique indicators to prevent the economic dilution within the market.

In the next phase, which includes the focus on neurological and behavioral therapies, it will become even more critical for members of the healthcare system to understand which portion of the value chain will be targeted. There are different strategies that can be employed by different players within the ecosystem, depending on what a specific focus is for differentiation in the space. Companies need to be smarter about their approach, in going after unique neurological permutations and utilise data driven together with an understanding of how the strategy will enable differentiation. For example, the competitive advantage could be focused on experience or the science together with the efficacy of using a device and therapy together or another approach could be a more generic and aggregate play.

The approach toward the creation of cardiovascular therapeutics, which is a very large market, lacked strategy by pharmaceutical companies and the market was crowded. The oncology market was much smaller in comparison, although the neurological and behavioural therapies represent a sizable market in the future. The addressable market and incidents rates will be much higher and will require a strategy driven by data to determine what strategies the pharmaceutical companies will choose to play out.

The data economy for the creation of pharmaceuticals and therapies requires a lot of tertiary data sets that are not internal datasets, from research at universities to the identification of target markets, diagnostics capabilities, therapeutic modality, to finally deploying a commercial product. Cellular and gene therapies are newly emerged approaches that evolved seven to eight years ago from universities. A growing amount of the data consumed is emerging from outside of the pharmaceutical companies. Provider networks, hospitals, and other members of the value chain will capture different amounts of value from the data which will need to be reflected in the data economy as the economics begin to shift.

Today the exchange for data is structured by pharmaceutical companies as commercial alliances and partnerships with the universities and labs with monetary. For example, the oncology therapeutic modality called Chimeric Antigen Receptor T-Cell Therapy, which came out of academia close to eight years ago and took a partnership with many pharmaceutical companies over many years that can cure cancer. These modified CAR T-Cell Receptor therapies have produced three therapies by different pharmaceutical companies. When you look at immunotherapy, it took about 40 years from the first research paper to the availability of a commercial drug. That cycle will get compressed, but this will require a shift on the use of data through academia, providers, patients, and healthcare providers.

In the EU, there is the development of a data trust for citizens to contribute data across the value chain with certain tax credits. GDPR has granted citizens the rights to their data, although as a citizen of the European Union that is receiving healthcare there is a duty to contribute individual data in scale for research. The bio banks are becoming popular, especially the UK which has captured one of the highest quality patient data.

Data companies like Flatiron Health, which organises cancer data gathered from a network of over 250 oncology practices, are creating valuable data assets useful in clinical trials, which is why it was acquired by Roche for $1.9 billion. This is clearly a direct monetisation of data play. Other pharmaceutical companies are more focused on the metrics around superior scientific approach in therapeutic outcomes in addressing significantly unmet needs of patient populations.

There are also many other dimensions of the data and different models. For example, the viability for multiple players, the metrics around how much value being captured within the value chain and the focus on specific dimensions within the value chain, offer different approaches. The question is also what is the role that the pharmaceutical company wants to play from data aggregator to data consumer.

The customer experience and journey for patients within healthcare ecosystems, extend beyond the specific treatments. Data plays a critical role throughout the healthcare ecosystem, yet today it is driven primarily by internal data with roughly only 20 per cent is external data from other segments and entities. The digital transformation of healthcare will drive the need to utilise more external data sources in the future, which will require a totally new approach in data sharing and frameworks for measuring the value creation driven by data within the economy. In the future, the various members of the healthcare ecosystems will need to agree on the metrics to enable all parties to benefit fairly from the value creation. The future through the transformation enabled through the data economy may be more about bartering than it is about a financial marketplace. The value for information needs to be understood, quantifiable, measurable, and tangible.

***

Chapter 8

# New Business and Revenue Models

As business is scaling, "platformation" of data monetisation is becoming critical. Modelling decisions with data, consuming the services of these models, and in turn creating a data driven business is no longer optional, it is a must.

The ability of a Chief Data Economy Officer (CDEO), to successfully transform an organisation around the needs of customers, utilising data from various parts of an ecosystem beyond the company or entity, requires a structure that has four main pillars:

**1) Business Model**

The business model needs to be defined with the customer at the center and a total understanding of the flow of data, incorporating all the vectors described in prior chapters. The customer benefits that will be derived and the resources associated with the delivery need to be correlated with the data and activities.

**2) Revenue and Pricing Model**

The value creation and associated revenue needs to be modelled to understand where revenue will be derived to accurately price the offering.

**3) New Enterprise Operating Model**

Redefining the business platforms and revolutionising business processes and services through technology and data can be transformational with the right structure and a CDEO. The customer journey and data flowing throughout the ecosystem need to be understood as central to the transformation.

**4) Consumption Model**

The customer is central to the modeling of a usage-based structure and how the services are provisioned and paid. New models offering new options for consumption of services have been transformative in enabling digital native startups to scale up and meet the needs of customers within the resource constraints of a young company. It enables faster time to market with greater flexibility than larger enterprises.

A simple definition of a business model can be drawn from Drucker's theory of business or Michael Porter's definition of strategy, as a way to define how the business will make money in the context of market needs, competitors, and the customer. Connectivity and distributed systems have decentralised these first-generation business models. Over the years, companies that were originally hardware or product companies have faced changing market dynamics and evolving customer needs, as the same old business models

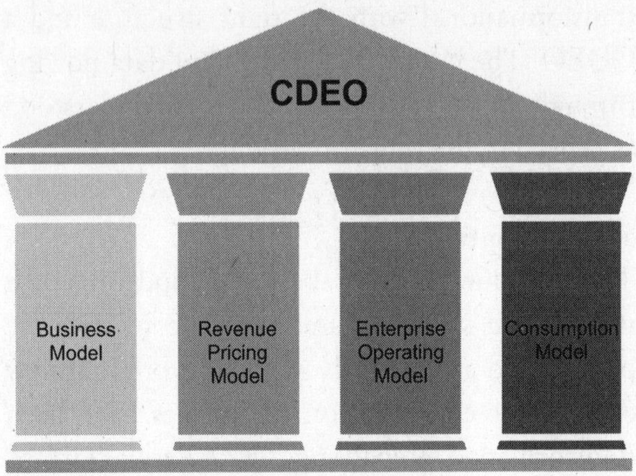


**Evolution of Business Models**

have stopped working, and new non-traditional competitive offerings have cannibalised the traditional market share of the original businesses.

Digital transformation requires revolutionised business models. There are many dimensions to digital transformation that have extended far beyond the data managed by the IT department. It involves data woven into supply chains, data extracted from touchpoints across customer journeys, or data that passes across ecosystems composed of partners. It is not a simple representation of a physical product within a simple market which is addressing static customer needs which are met specifically within the constraints of the business. The question is how these entities should be modelled to better define the business which extends beyond traditional barriers.

### Main Components of Traditional Business Models

One more recent tool that has evolved to help map, design, and discuss new business models is called the Business Model Canvas; it has nine key building blocks which include key partners, key activities, key resources, value propositions, customer relationships, channels, customer segments, cost structure and revenue streams.

Each section has a specific hypothesis that is developed by working through the questions to understand the various aspects.

The customer centric Business Model Canvas shown above, by Alexander Osterwalder and Yves Pigneur, offers a different approach from the first-generation business models. It utilises nine building blocks which enable companies to move beyond the product approach to focus on the business model. Transformations from transactions (or product sales into relationships) that offer recurring revenue streams required a different approach. This included the ability to lay out all the different dependencies associated with setting up a distribution channel.

This canvas identifies the key drivers of a business and how they fit together on one sheet of paper. There is a customer focus embedded within what it takes to deliver the value to the customer, and it is easy to understand the connections and dependencies. It helps identify the target customer base, the revenue sources, products, and cost to begin to visualise the key business elements. Yet this is not enough for a data driven business. In addition to the customer centric approach, there needs to be an understanding of the data.

**KEY PARTNERS**

Who are our key partners?
Who are our key suppliers?
Which key resources are we acquiring from our partners?
Which key activities do partners perform?

**CHANNELS**

Through which channels do our customer segments want to be reached?
How do other companies reach them now?
Which ones work best? Which ones are most cost-efficient?
How are we integrating them with customer routines?

**KEY ACTIVITIES**

What key activities do our value propositions require?
Our distribution channels?
Customer relationships?
Revenue streams?

**KEY RESOURCES**

What key resources do our value propositions require?
Our distribution channels?
Customer relationships?
Revenue streams?

**COST STRUCTURE**

What are the most important costs inherent to our business model?
Which key resources are most expensive?
Which key activities are most expensive?

**VALUE PROPOSITIONS**

What value do we deliver to the customer?
Which one of our customers' problems are we helping to solve?
What bundles of products and services are we offering to each segment?
Which customer needs are we satisfying?
What is the minimum viable product?

**CUSTOMER RELATIONSHIPS**

How do we get, keep, and grow customers?
Which customer relationships have we established?
How are they integrated with the rest of our business model?
How costly are they?

**CUSTOMER SEGMENTS**

For whom are we creating value?
Who are our most important customers?
What are the customer archetypes?

**REVENUE STREAMS**

For what value are our customers really willing to pay? For what do they currently pay?
What is the revenue model?
What are the pricing tactics?

**Business Model Canvas**

## Desirability, Feasibility and Viability (DVF) of Data Economy Models

Many entrepreneurs that pitch their products to investors start with a bold statement about the value of all the data they are capturing. Few companies know how to extract value to serve customer needs. While it is far easier to launch a digitally native company to provide new business models on a blank slate, it can be resource-intensive to build and grow an entity based on the insights gathered from the data. Not all data is valuable, and most data needs work to extract value.

### Desirability

Desirability is defined from the traditional customer journey and experience with a product or services. In using the DVF approach, it is important to understand the desirability by the customer and the pain point that the solution is addressing. A customer does not want to experience downtime in business and wants a service that guarantees a higher level of business productivity.

### Feasibility

Mimicking a business model that works for one industry, may not always be appropriate for other industries. Innovation should strengthen the competitive advantage of the business or increase their customer engagement.

**Viability**

While viability may be the hardest of the three to test, it is the most critical to enable long-term sustained growth. The services need to enhance customer engagement and revenue growth.

Understanding the Desirability, Feasibility and Viability (DVF) of the chosen model creates important constraints the model must focus on and that will enable the business to grow using data.

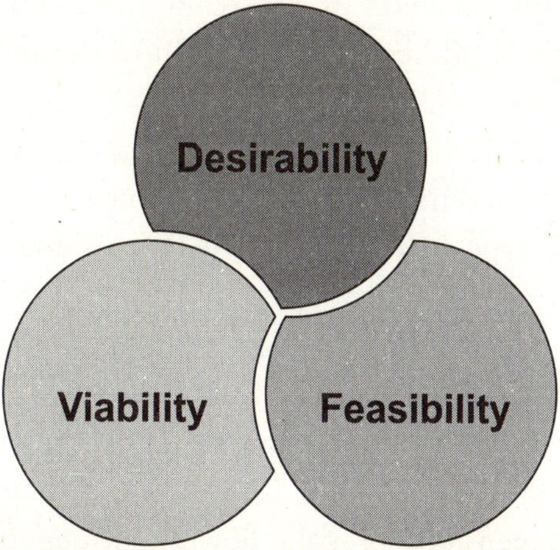


**Consumer View of All Four Models**

Modelling the Data Driven Business Model requires looking at a business canvas from a completely different perspective. The data needs to be at the center of the model, and the relationships with the data need to be defined specific to the use case to understand the purpose, the participants, the data products and the economics around the data usage and contributions. The diagram below tries to offer a different type of canvas worksheet to work through the economics for the data driven business. Data is central to the model and all the elements involved in the economic evaluation need to be addressed to fuel the flow throughout the ecosystem.

Data Driven Business Models are driven by the data and not the customer journey. It enables a new type of relationship with customers, by powering new types of flexible business models.

Understanding the Data journey and the role of the data is critical. The Data Economy Canvas below offers a template for the CDEO to model out the data economy, by working through all the dimensions of data flowing throughout a given organisation.

#### Consumer of Data (Consumption Model)

The consumers of the data in the data economy frame the use case for the business model. A

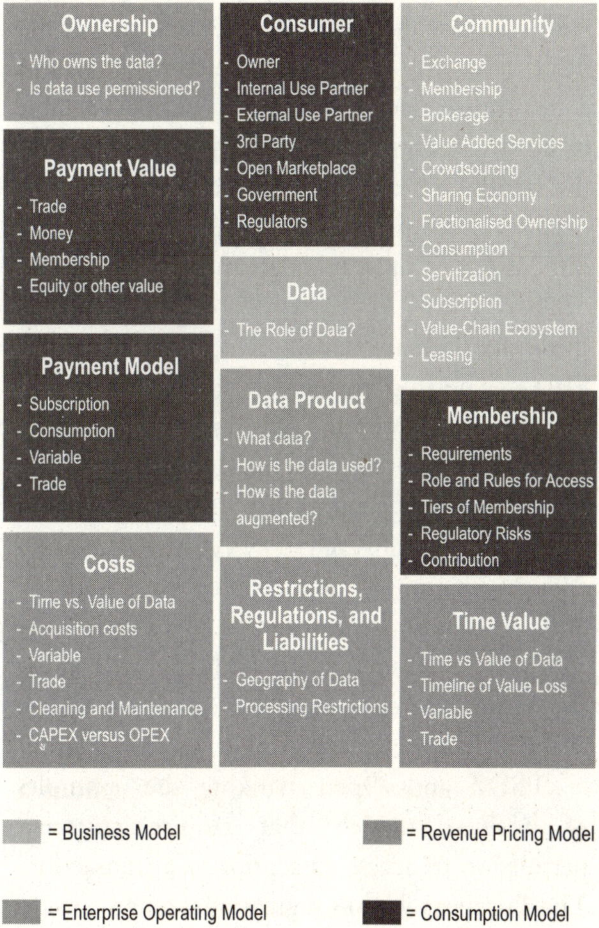
Ownership
- Who owns the data?
- Is data use permissioned?
Consumer
- Owner
- Internal Use Partner
- External Use Partner
- 3rd Party
- Open Marketplace
- Government
- Regulators
Community
- Exchange
- Membership
- Brokerage
- Value Added Services
- Crowdsourcing
- Sharing Economy
- Fractionalised Ownership
- Consumption
- Servitization
- Subscription
- Value-Chain Ecosystem
- Leasing
Payment Value
- Trade
- Money
- Membership
- Equity or other value
Data
- The Role of Data?
Payment Model
- Subscription
- Consumption
- Variable
- Trade
Data Product
- What data?
- How is the data used?
- How is the data augmented?
Membership
- Requirements
- Role and Rules for Access
- Tiers of Membership
- Regulatory Risks
- Contribution
Costs
- Time vs. Value of Data
- Acquisition costs
- Variable
- Trade
- Cleaning and Maintenance
- CAPEX versus OPEX
Restrictions, Regulations, and Liabilities
- Geography of Data
- Processing Restrictions
Time Value
- Time vs Value of Data
- Timeline of Value Loss
- Variable
- Trade
= Business Model
= Revenue Pricing Model
= Enterprise Operating Model
= Consumption Model

data economy created for a financial exchange will look very different from the one created for healthcare. Yet, there are correlations in which a healthcare data economy might be valuable to institutional traders looking to understand the trends in healthcare. The consumers of data may vary within each ecosystem, offering new dimensions of value to a data marketplace.

**Ownership (Revenue Model)**

Data ownership needs to be defined and understood to support each business model. In some instances, like the automobile industry, the distribution channel has many steps which capture data within each silo. In contrast, Tesla is a data-driven company with a deep understanding of its customers. Data is central to Tesla, it is the competitive advantage, in addition to owning the customer relationships. It has end-to-end visibility from manufacturing to customer sales.

PSD2 and Open Banking are examples of business models that require customer permission to access data prior to a transaction. The European Union regulations define citizens as the owners of their healthcare data, which is not the case in the United States.

**Payment Value (Consumption Model)**

The economics around data are related to the roles each entity plays in an ecosystem, which was presented earlier in this book. There are many forms of payments, from simple trading to payment transactions. The payments depend on membership roles and rules for access as well as the type of community that is being created around the data usage. Some members could have an equity stake in the ecosystem, in exchange for data and services.

**Payment Model (Consumption Model)**

The model for payments will be dependent on the type of community, the role within the community and the payment value that is placed on the data.

**Costs (Revenue Model)**

The cost of acquiring, cleaning, joining, storing, securing, computing, and analysing data can be very expensive, especially if the data is not needed. It is one of the aspects of data that is often overlooked. Over time, data loses value and not all data needs to be stored for extended periods of time. All companies have limited resources.

Focusing on resources that do not add value can be a distraction, in addition to being a resource drain.

#### Data Product (Enterprise Model)

The definition of what data is captured, productised, made available and augmented will depend on how the data is used. For example, neighbourhood traffic data for retail store location evaluation will have a completely different operational process when compared to the acquisition and use of aggregated and anonymised healthcare data. The ability to correlate an orthogonal data set, to add value to data, is a process that is not a requirement for all use cases.

Data can have many vectors that need to be understood in context of the data product being offered to the community.

#### Restrictions, Regulations and Liabilities (Enterprise Model)

The data liabilities and restrictions have been growing as the value of data across all industries grows exponentially. Financial institutions have restrictions on the use of customer data that is internal within their own systems. European Countries restrict the use or processing of certain types of data. For example, Ireland's

Data Protection Commission sent a preliminary order to Facebook ordering a suspension of data transfer from the EU to the US.

Financial institutions need to adhere to consumer protection laws and regulations. In the United States, there are Fair Lending laws that prohibit the use of certain types of data to prevent discrimination in offering lending, credit, or other financial products. The Equal Credit Opportunity Act prohibits any kind of discrimination associated with credit transactions, and the Fair Housing Act prohibits discrimination in residential real estate transactions.

### Time Value of Data (Revenue Model)

Over time, data will lose its value, but some types of data will remain a liability and maintaining data has costs. The strategy should never be to obtain every piece of data available just because it is accessible, data needs to have a purpose within the ecosystem. Some data is only valuable within milliseconds of a consumer action; other data may have value for decades. Data needs to be captured within the appropriate context. Web searches for a bathing suit or a camera prior to a vacation will generate unwanted ads for an extended period.

The data about the consumer's interest continues to be used even after a purchase has been made.

### Membership (Consumption Model)

All ecosystems have formal or informal members that transact and share information. The roles that were discussed in a prior chapter define how members participate in the ecosystem. The type of community is also a factor in defining how the members come together to transact and share information. For example, in some regulated environments, governments or regulatory entities may require access to data and transactions, making them a default partner in the echo ecosystem. The Anti Money Laundering legislation requires transactional information based on specified criteria.

### Community (Business Model)

There are many business models that bring together multisided platforms of producers and consumers. The data that fuels these business models is extremely valuable. It can transform a product company into a service company with stronger customer relations and insights. It can enable companies to have additional revenue streams that provide a constant and predictable cash flow. There is tremendous variability between all the different models, and the level of data, and transparency within the ecosystem.

The different Community models offer different types of marketplaces that adapt to the customer needs for a particular type of service.

**Application of Business Models**

Transformations that utilise data need a slightly different framework to map out the value generation and the ecosystem to create a business model. Value creation requires a customer centric journey and approach by mapping out the business model to break down the business model into the service components.

| | LOW | MEDIUM | HIGH |
|---|---|---|---|
| What is the value of the data? | | | |
| What is the force multiplier on sharing data? | | | |
| What is the cost of obtaining data? | | | |
| What is the cost of maintaining the data? | | | |
| What liabilities does the data represent? | | | |
| Who owns the data? | | | |
| What restrictions exist on data use? | | | |
| What geographic restrictions to process? | | | |
| What is the half-life rate of the data value? | | | |
| What is the growth rate of data? | | | |

The new business models that are fuelled by data are sourced through a variety of different entities, technologies, devices, processes, and contributors, that extend beyond the boundaries of a traditional business. The example of a data value assessment below identifies parameters that are critical to a business model that is driven by data, especially models that are customer centric.

#### Servitization

Some of the common next generation business models include servitization, which is the move from a product focus towards a subscription model which increases customer interaction, loyalty, and insights. A study from McKinsey indicates that a new product may only have a 10 per cent profit margin, while aftermarket services can average 25 per cent margins.

This move also requires utilising data to perform the services within the length of the customer contract. A 2018 North American study by the IFS indicated that only four per cent of the respondents were offering full servitization of production through a subscription service and not through usage fee agreements. The servitization-centered economy has enabled manufacturing companies to shift from a single product focus, to a more customer centric relationship with improved customer service opportunities. This shift requires understanding the data that is generated through this new business model to strengthen customer relationships.

For example, Apple moved to offer Apple One as a tiered subscription that includes Apple Music, Apple Arcade, Apple TV, Apple News, and iCloud, versus selling individual digital media products through its store. Disney+ launched a service which enabled them to connect directly with its customers through its service and learn from their interactions.

### Platforms

"Platformation" has grown in popularity and promoted the use of platforms to power exchanges for price discovery or to enable the shared economy. Platforms connect businesses, communities, and customers. While these platform models do not manufacture products or own assets like real estate, automobiles, or equipment that can be utilised or rented out by community members, it provides connectivity between the producers and the consumers of a variety of products and services.

These platforms can offer communities a marketplace for price discovery for services that are offered as consumers explore and bid on the offerings based on specific criteria. There are many forms of platforms that are created to offer digital services including communities, marketplaces, distribution platforms, content, transactional and financial services. They are powered by data, which is continuously harvested and joined to increase value and functionality for the consumers of the services.

#### Next Generation Data Driven

Data Driven business models are evolving and provide many new ways to service customers at different points in a customer journey. Financial services are now offered seamlessly within the context of a transaction, using data to quickly increase the speed at which customers can transact, while providing the financial firm with new customers at lower acquisition costs than traditional media or digital advertising platforms offer.

Data Driven business models can improve the customer journey, offering efficiencies to customers, the platforms and financial lending firms. These integrated offerings utilise data to understand the needs and risks and expedite decisions, financing, and customer engagement.

In today's rising regulatory climate, the journeys of customers, transactions, processes, and products over time and across ecosystems are a growing requirement. The European MiFID II and the Anti-money Laundering directives are examples of data requirements that need to be captured from different sources within the ecosystem and presented upon request for regulatory compliance. Networked ecosystems need to support the data driven economy as well as the regulatory requirements that will drive adoption and transformation.

## OUTSIDE-IN VIEW

### 1) Revenue and Pricing Models

The Pricing and Revenue that can be generated by data within an ecosystem through the offered services requires a level of insight to analyse the opportunity from the perspective of the consumer. This allows the organisation to understand the what, why, and how in the value creation to create a revenue model.

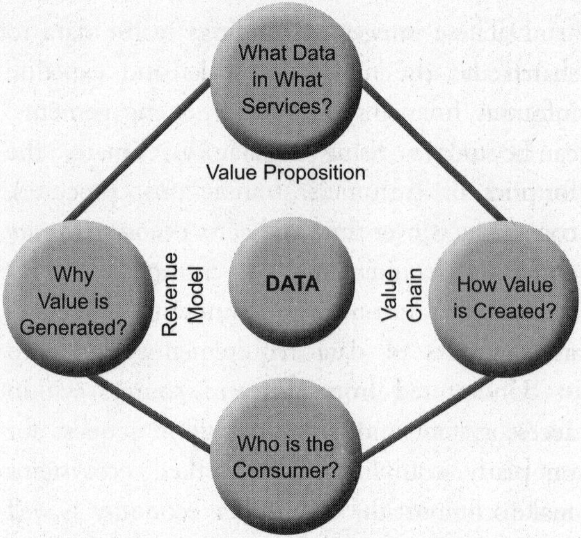


**2) New Enterprise and Operating Models**

The new enterprise and operating models that can evolve from the business model analysis can incorporate just one of the different types of communities listed on the Data Driven Model Canvas. The servitization model, which enables a product manufacturing company to transform to a service company by offering new data driven services is now being adopted across many different industries. Not all data has the same value, and not all communities can utilise the same types of marketplaces.

Data is fueling the new business models. The shared economy is enabled by a platform that offers information from owners or service providers that can be searched by consumers. There is a method for price discovery within specific parameters, and consumers can register to access the information about the use of a property or the availability of a service which enables them to select and transact at a desired point in time.

Understanding how consumers want to access a service, or utilise a resource, can evolve on platforms as more users enter queries and make selections.

Crowdsourcing and open-source models have become much more popular over the past two decades. Companies, like Red Hat, have even built layered services above open-source models. Rolls Royce offered 'Power-by-the-Hour service in 1962 which revolutionised the fixed-cost-per-flying hour concept' Customers want services that enable an increase in product availability to improve business performance and would pay more for these services, yet according to Worldwide Business Research (WBR) only 33 per cent of manufacturers were offering these types of services in 2018.

The Data Economy offers members the

opportunity to develop a closer relationship with customers and suppliers through new types of business models.

**3) Consumption Models**

The opportunity to service customers through new consumption models will grow with edge computing. The architectures to support data sharing are evolving to support many types of communities and consumption models.

Assuming the data economy is enabled on a cloud platform and not on premise, here are a few examples for the 3rd Party Marketplace, Derived Information, Hybrid Premise/Cloud, New Segments and OEM.

Exchanges, Value Added Services, Crowd-Sourcing, Shared Economy, Fractional Ownership, Servitization, Subscription, Value-Chain Ecosystems and Leasing are just a few of the many models that are powered by platforms that consume data for price discovery and categorisation.

The growth of consumption models fuelled by data will require an investment in data-driven technologies, visibility throughout supply chains, and insights on customer journeys. Complex models evolve through the analysis of demand

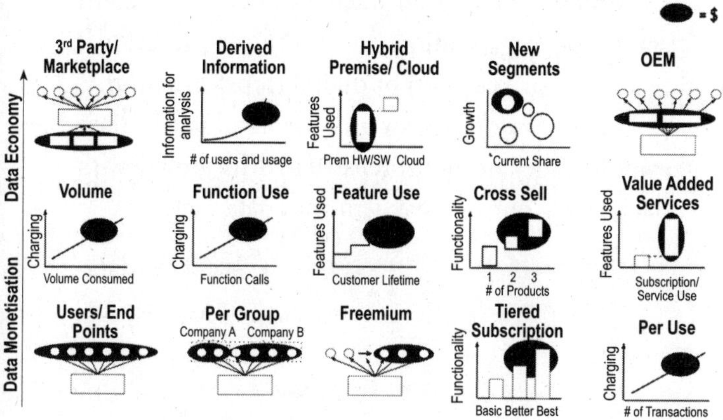


based on other factors that enable more profitable services, whereas peak demand may correlate with a premium value a customer may be willing to pay.

The customer relationship is being redefined using data, and customers are willing to pay for the increased value. Engaging with a customer through a service, provides greater opportunities to grow the relationship.

#### Digital Maturity in Business Modelling

Understanding the digital maturity of an organisation is an important step for organisations looking to transform, utilising one of the different community business models to service their customers. The example below shows the different stages of organisations and the organisational readiness for adoption of digital transformation.

Once an organisation has evaluated their standing, they are more prepared to drive growth with data, laying out an ecosystem with data exchange.

***

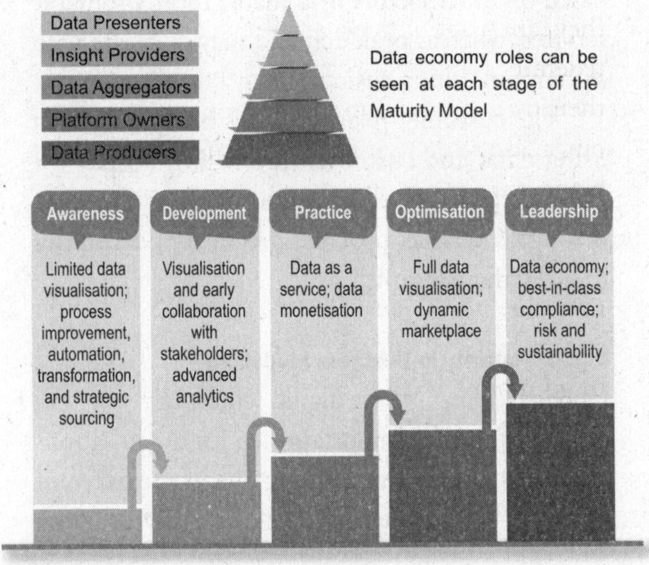

Chapter 9

# Changing Industry Boundaries within Specific Verticals

Organisations, while inventing, innovating, and discovering new commercials models, are in a rise to transform their branding and go to market, they are continuously thinking about how to redefine, and when to redefine the boundaries of their own organisations. This is critical to figure out at this juncture as the whole value chain is being under tight scrutiny especially after the pandemic.

While organisations are still figuring out their nonvalue added steps to be removed via value stream mapping exercise, the leaders are thinking to go more horizontally while creating a seamless integration vertically. One of the key thoughts is to redefine their data strategy, IP strategy and compatibility strategy. To achieve this, a strong infrastructure with built-in threat models must exist. Knowing where they are in the data economy is key (ABCD Triangle) to redefine the boundaries. Let us take a few industry sectors and depict the state of the art in data economy space.

Keeping collaboration and competition in mind, a large industrial and manufacturing and distribution company is taking steps to play a critical role in changing the boundaries of their organisation with their partners. Siemens (public information) is one of the first movers in the B2B space who is driving sustainable/green products go to market strategies. They are compelling all products (new, refurbished, returns, scraps) to have a call home feature to exactly pinpoint where a particular product is sitting in the ecosystem.

Sustainability is not an option but a must for an organisation's earning per share value. To drive a sustainable value chain, strategising open economy between tier one, two and three suppliers, the organisation itself (in this case Siemens) and forward distributors and dealers becomes a mandate.

Platform Partnership Alliance: A significant area to investigate prior to deciding the boundary lines, is platform strategy. A platform can be of various types. It could be of a type where one organisation owns it and creates contributor and consumer models, or it can be a brokered platform, or it can be a proprietary platform with insights to be bought by the consumers.

Creating a friendly alliance model to sell and buy data can be a boom to the revenue stream. Creating a broker model where members can upload and download data would be another way of delivering value.

**Platform partnership Alliance**

- Define ownership boundaries
- Establish key milestones based on input from legal
- Define name/branding
- Secure trademark
- Define revenue sharing model
- Confirm investment funding sources to build out the marketplace

**On-board ecosystem partners**

- Identify specific target partners
- Develop marketing communication to solicit their engagement including a specific ROI

**Commercial Model Definition**

- Compile cost estimate to build and maintain platform and associated ecosystem
- Develop business case of associated benefits to be realised by customers/stakeholders
- Define go to market cost and pricing strategies

**Customer/Stakeholder Definition**

- Capture key stakeholder groups within the jobsite ecosystem
- Refine initial hypothesis for value creation for unique entities/personas
- Utilise Design Thinking workshop to define key personas, associated use cases and
- Reach out to initial target stakeholder groups and gage their interest

**Technology**

- Capture data input requirements (e.g. machine data, worker data, weather, production schedule, commodity market data, etc.)
- Identity contributing sources of input (sensors, systems, third party data, etc.)
- Define model and method to ingest the data (e.g. telematics, apis, etc.)
- Define analytical and cognitive capability requirements
- Platform architecture

Customer/Stakeholde Definition: Boundaries are getting blurry for a better business outcome through external stakeholders participating during critical decisions by the organisation. Clearly defining the network of influence is becoming more and more critical.

Technology: Can we live without technology anymore? The answer is no. We cannot. We just need to realise where we are now in our own individual journey maps and create a calculated risk to commit to bold moves in technology space. One key area is to participate in data economy.

Commercial Model Definition: As talked in the previous chapter, B2B2C, B2C2B, C2B2B are becoming common in the value chain. Fin-Tech being the pioneer in driving a B2C mindset in all aspects of financial business, other sectors are not behind either. They are all adopting the B2C mindshare. Question is if they are all ready. They will be. If they adopt the open data economy space.

On-Board Ecosystem Partners: Onboarding partners in the open economy will be a critical move. As industry boundaries are getting blurry, sectors like Industrial, Life Sciences, Distribution and Logistics are all shifting to low touch onboarding experience.

Overall having a robust governance structure would mitigate the risk and enable compliance. This will drive more of an open economy which will create green zones for business. This whole process will demand a data economy which is flexible, reliable, and sustainable. Establishing a data centric canvas (leveraging ABCD Framework shown in previous chapter) will drive better decision-making power by the leaders. Fintech's "KYC" has new normal definitions now. "C" may now stand for Contract, Care or Consensus besides "Customer". Have you noticed it?

It's all about experience-led, data-led, and prediction-led models. Once you bring the customer to the forefront, customer as your key strategy to win, a data led economy becomes an enabler.

Having a CDEO at the helm is where the organisations will witness the most change. Automatically, opening the boundaries of the organisations, creating passcodes to the value chain gates known by certain roles in the value chain, wanting to enable sustainable growth, and finally, embracing sustainability to mitigate risk will only be possible once the leaders embrace a strategic role in the data economy. As the world witnesses Environmental, Social and Governance

(ESG) regulations becoming the key pillar for next generation transformation along with AI, CDEO is the new CEO.

You better know where you are in the ABCD Data Economy triangle.

Let us go deep into the ESG transformation in the next series where audience will apply the ABCD Data Economy triangle. At the end its all about monetisation of data!

***

# About the Authors

**Anirban, 'Andy,' Bhattacharyya** has over twenty years of experience in strategy, research, development, and implementation of next-generation transformation programs. His reach has spanned sustainability, supply chain, manufacturing, industrial internet of things and customer experience. After studying engineering at Birla Institute of Technology and Science, India, Andy earned an MBA in strategy and marketing from the Fuqua School of Business at Duke University. He founded Amplo Global Inc. in 2018, an artificial intelligence led Sustainability Risk Analysis organisation which has transformed the way an organisation executes risk management and carbon accounting through data strategy. He serves as the head of Sustainability for HPE Services Group. Andy is a Sustainability leader, Climate risk advisor, Forbes author, Patent holder, TedX speaker and Advisor to technology startups.

**Cristina Dolan** is an MIT alumna, engineer, entrepreneur, and thought leader focused on building and growing businesses utilising data and advanced technologies to build new digitally transformative fintech, insurtech and mobility offerings. She is a Co-Founder of Additum, an award winning European Value Based Healthcare ecosystem utilising data feedback to motivate patient outcomes. Christiana has been working on cybersecurity, and the frameworks for protecting data as a board advisory to three award winning companies focused on different aspects of cybersecurity. Earlier, she has led product management for trading data products at SaaS software company. She also co-founded OneMain, which grew to be one of the largest Internet Service Provider. In addition to executive roles at IBM and Oracle bringing new products to market, Cristina was CEO of venture backed MIT spinoff WordStream. Most recently, she has been working on cybersecurity, and the frameworks for protecting data as a board advisory to three award winning companies focused on different aspects of cybersecurity. Currently, she is the Managing Director for LATAM at RSA Security. She is also TEDx speaker and keynote speaker.